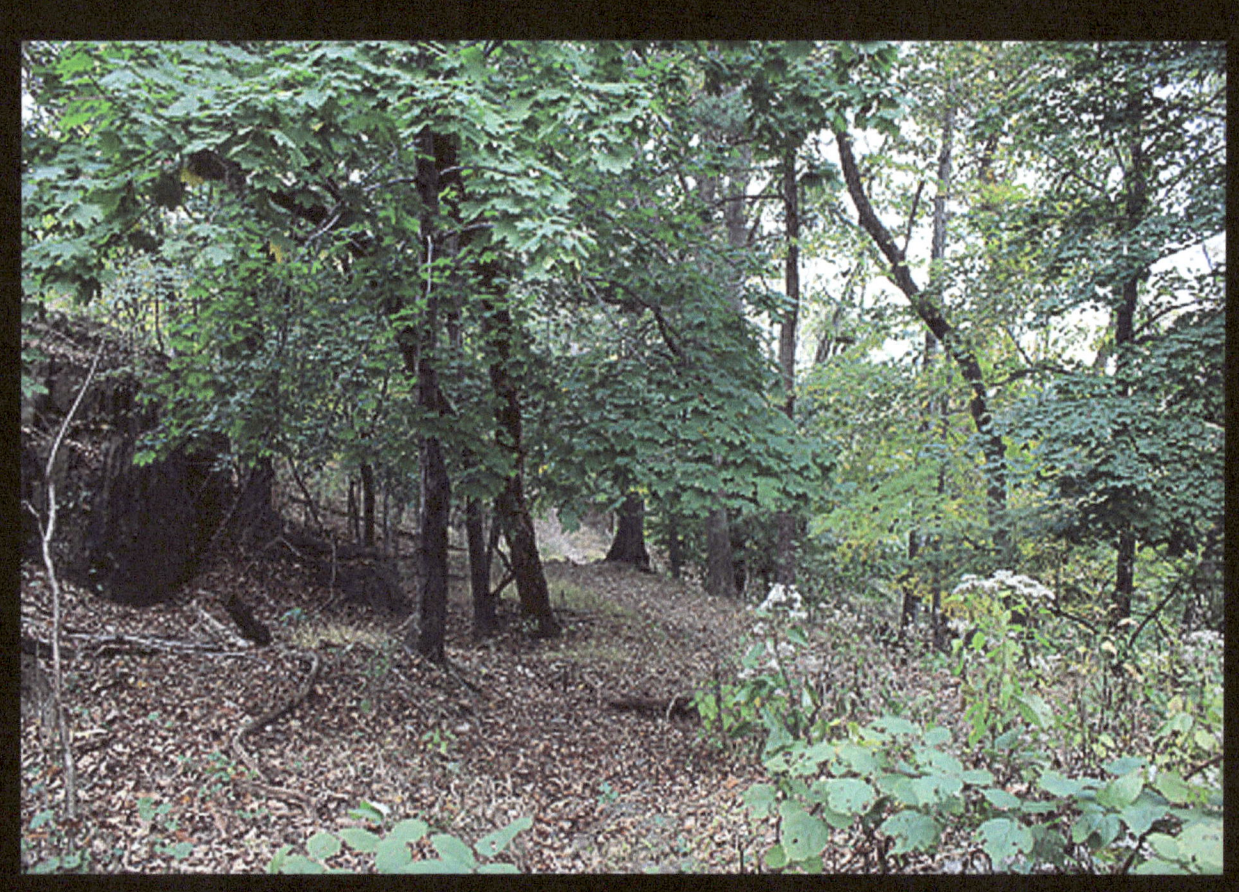

EAGLE ROCK RESERVATION

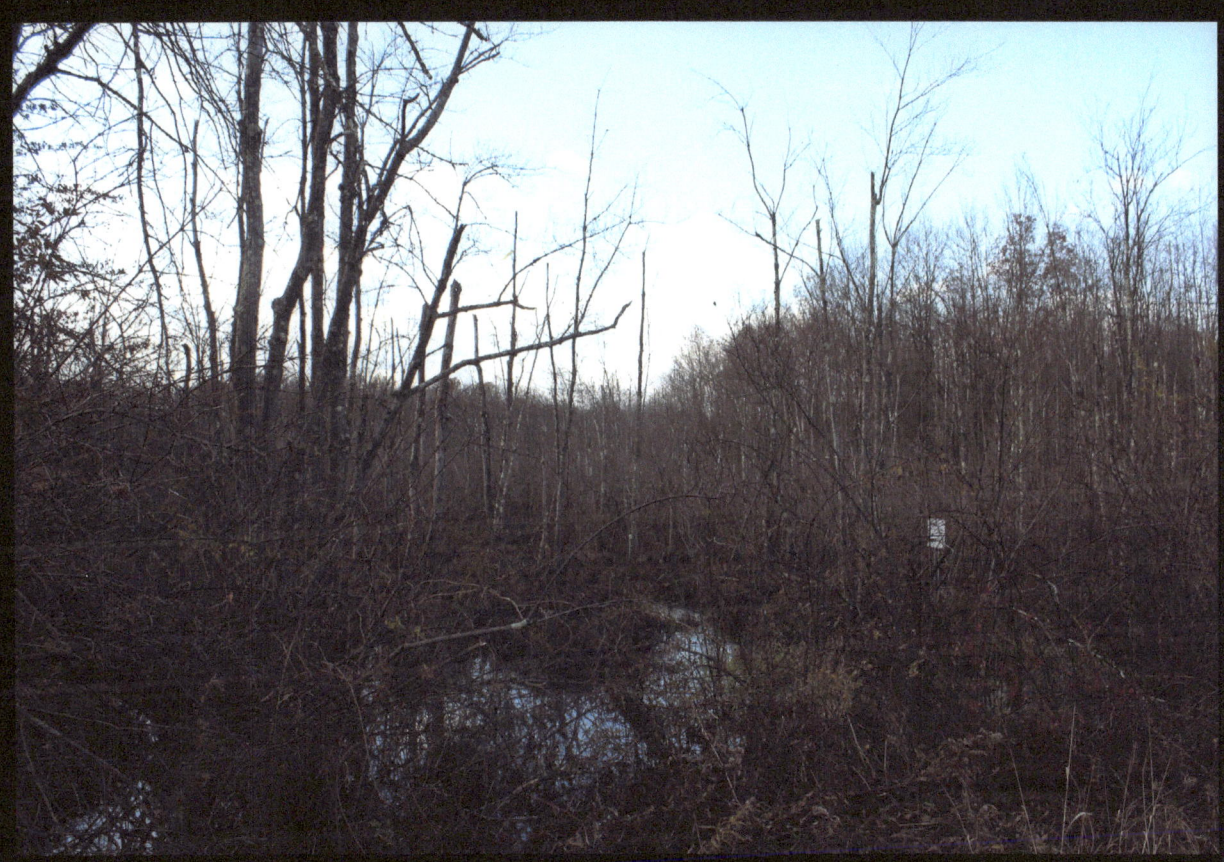

GREAT SWAMP WILDLIFE REFUGE

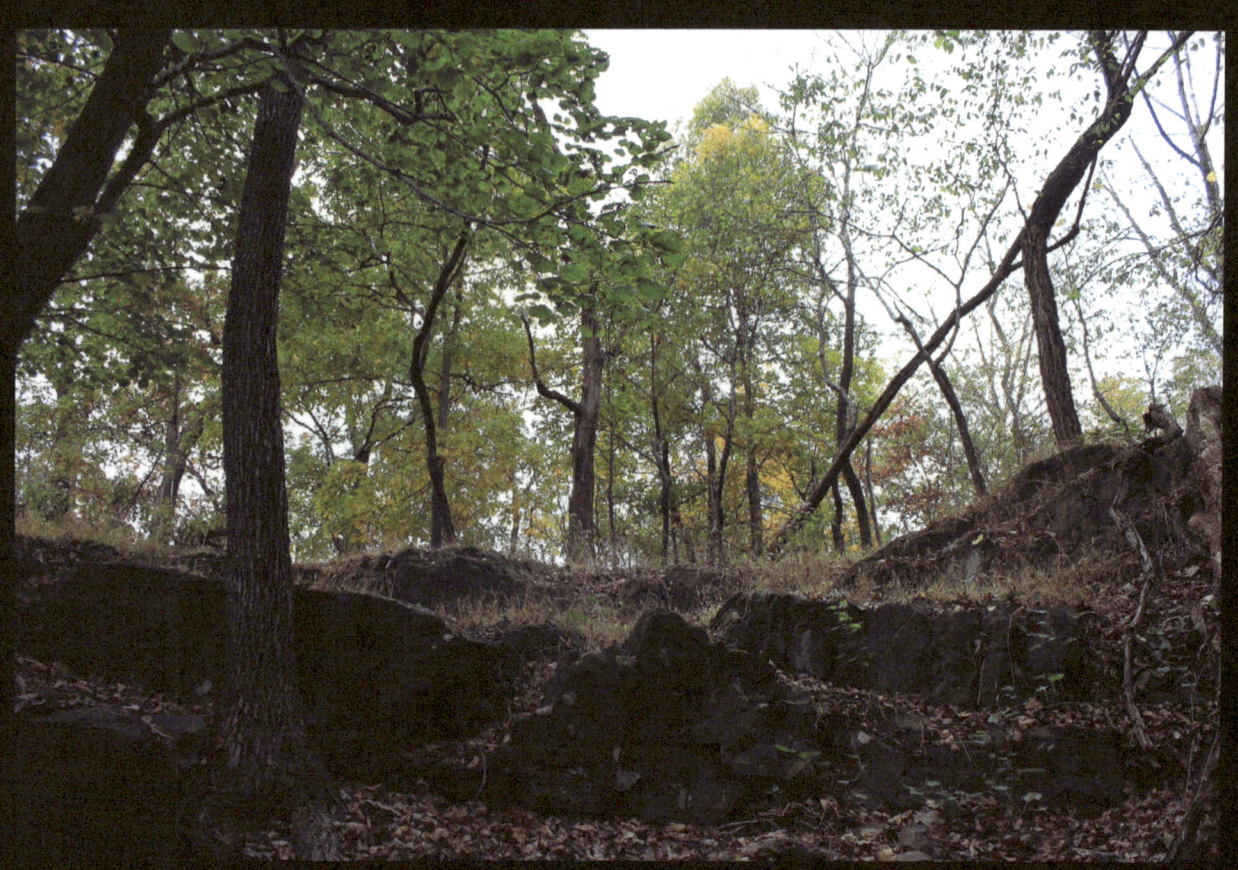

EAGLE ROCK RESERVATION

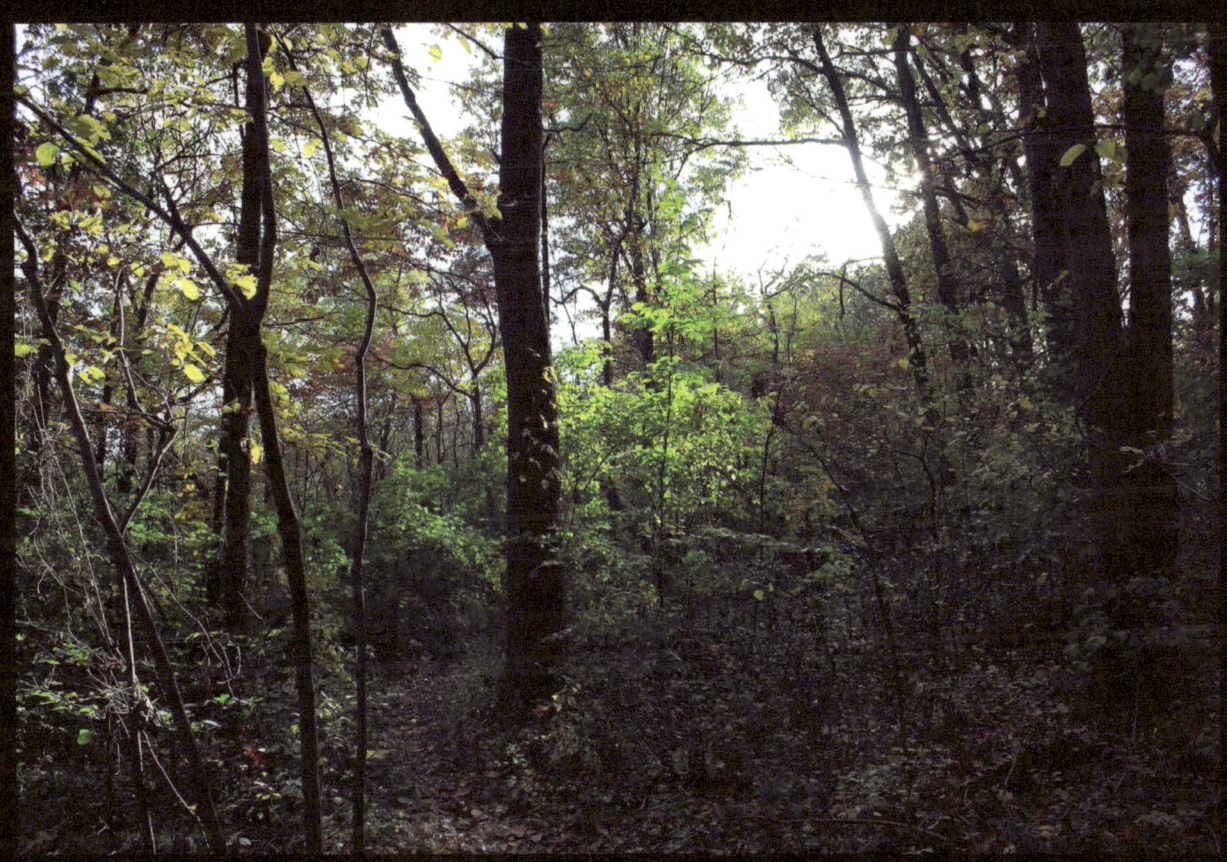

WATCHUNG RESERVATION

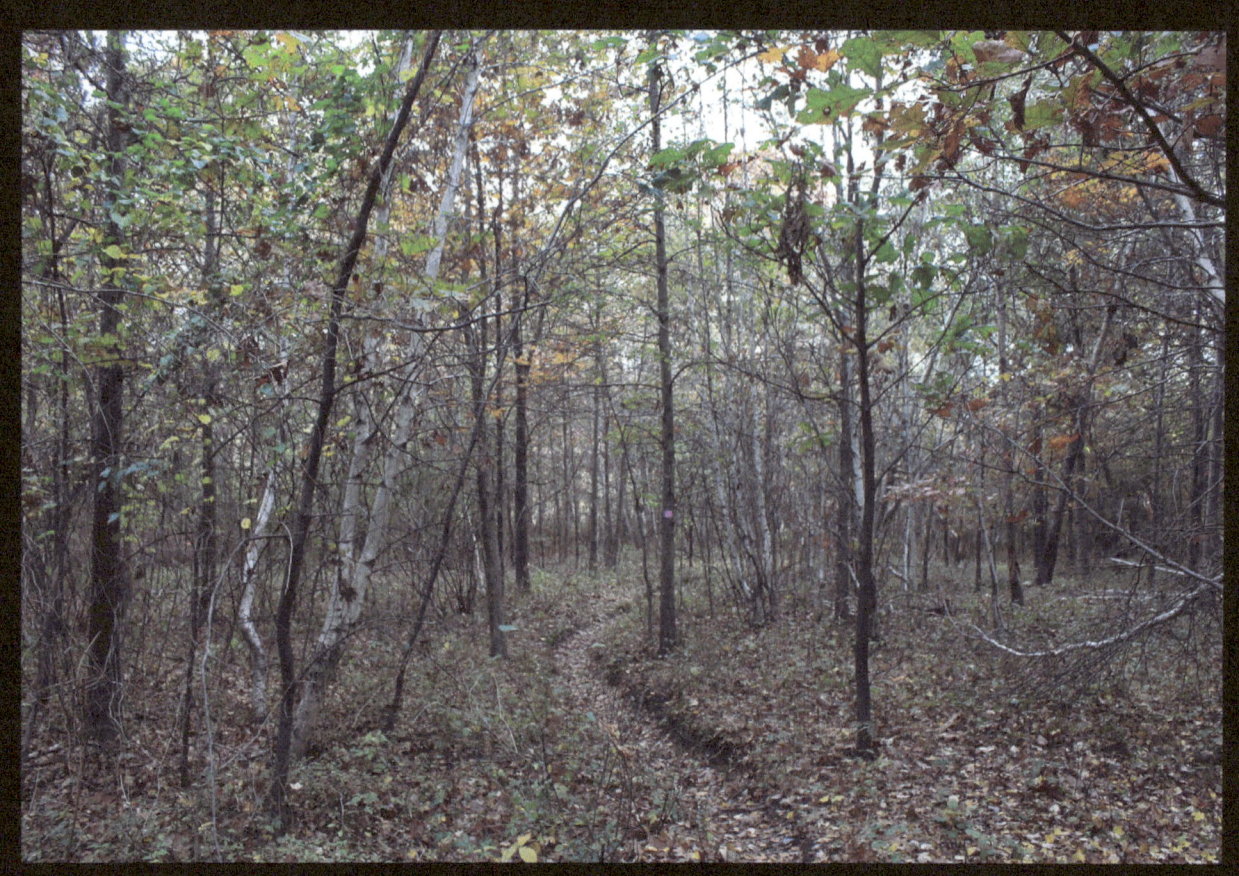

WATCHUNG RESERVATION

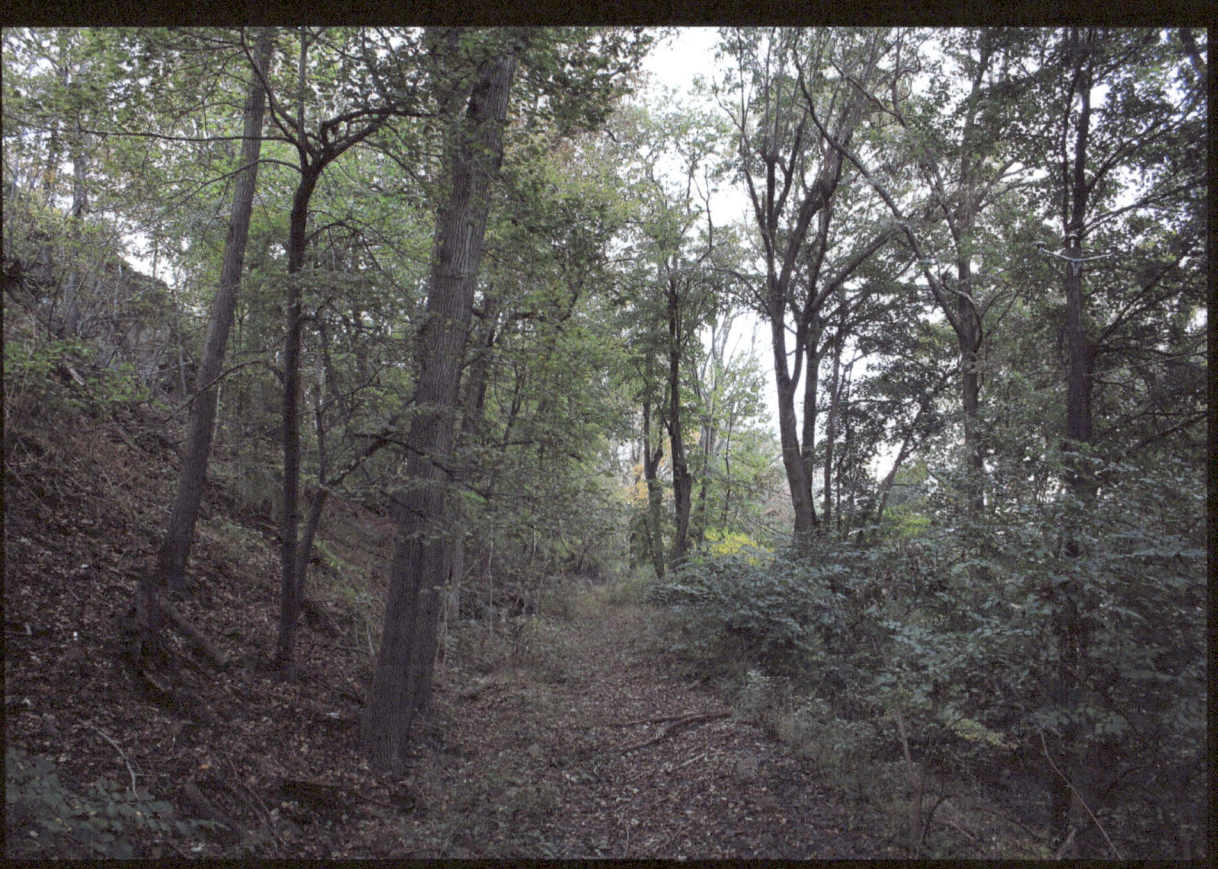

EAGLE ROCK RESERVATION

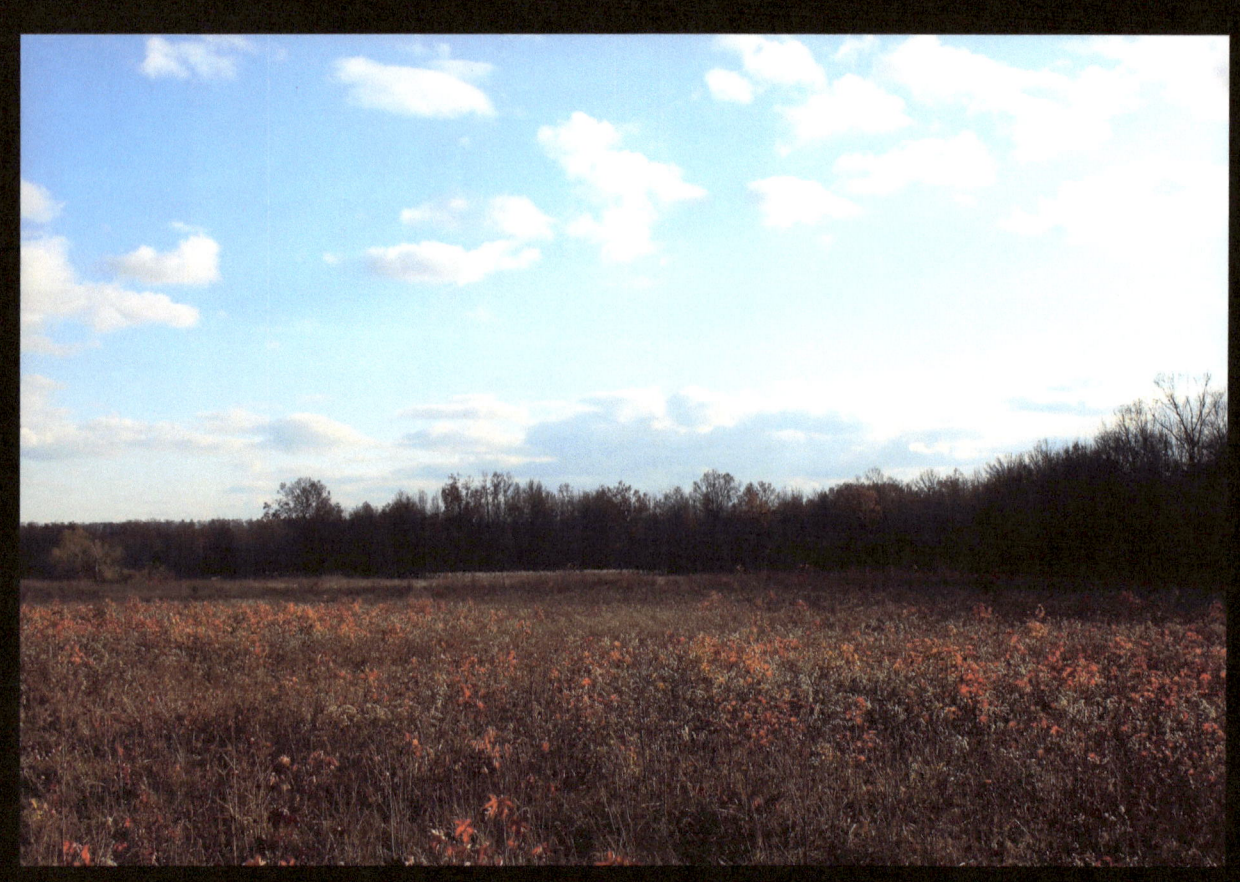

GREAT SWAMP WILDLIFE REFUGE

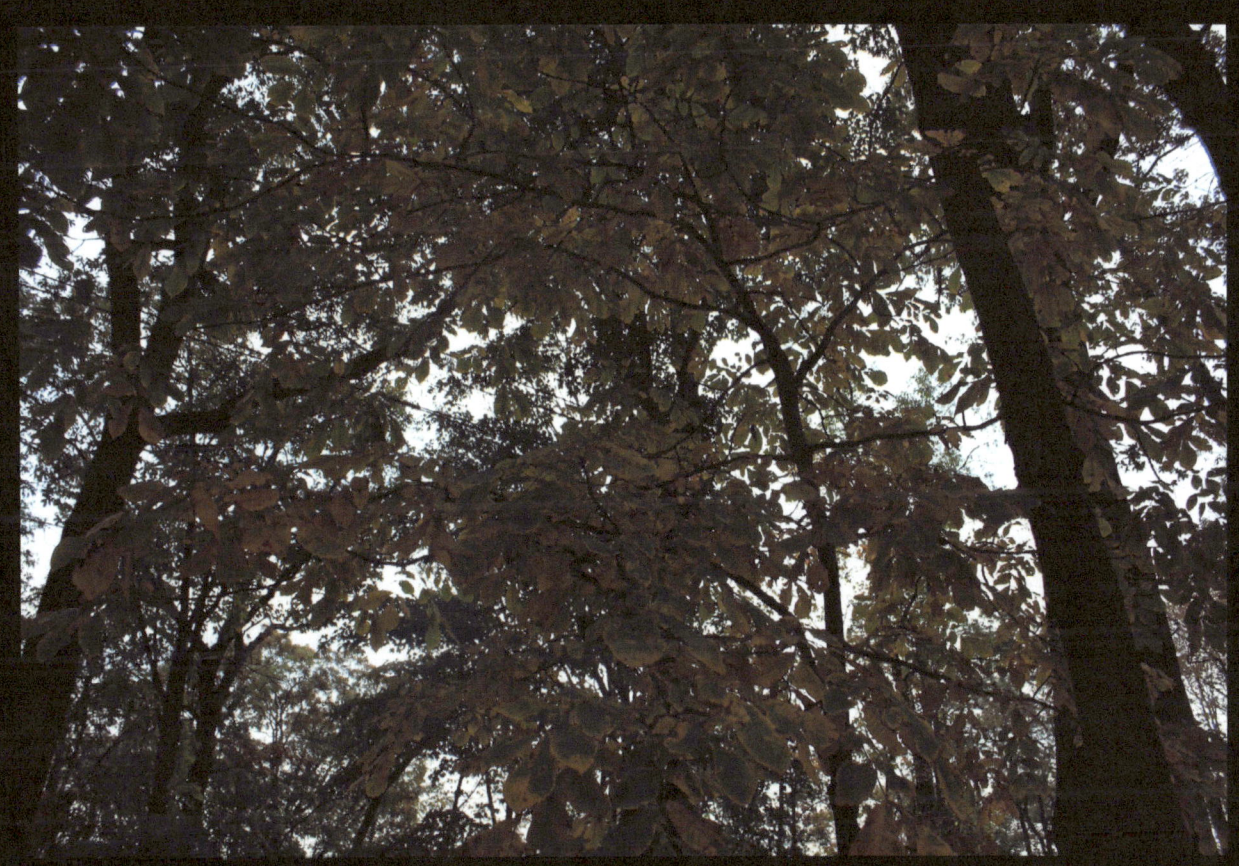

EAGLE ROCK RESERVATION

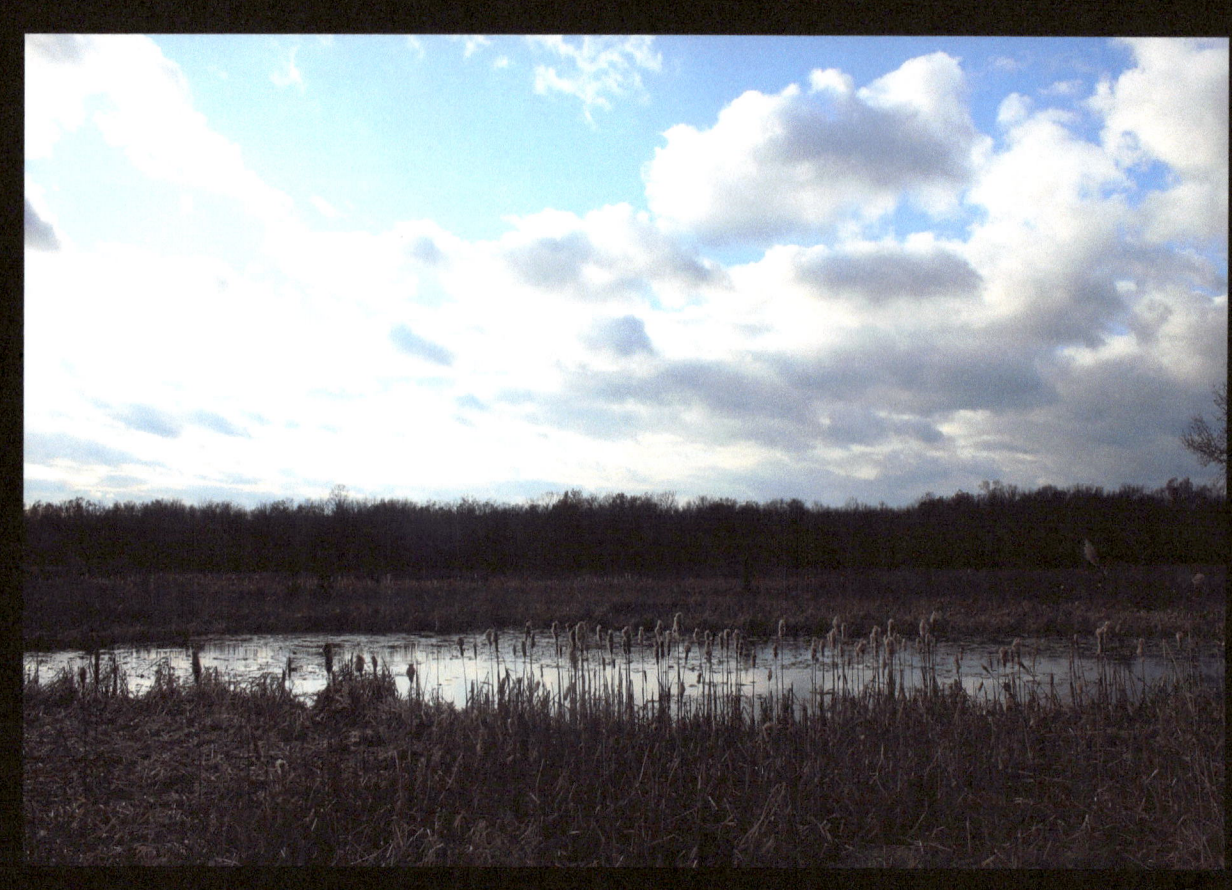

GREAT SWAMP WILDLIFE REFUGE

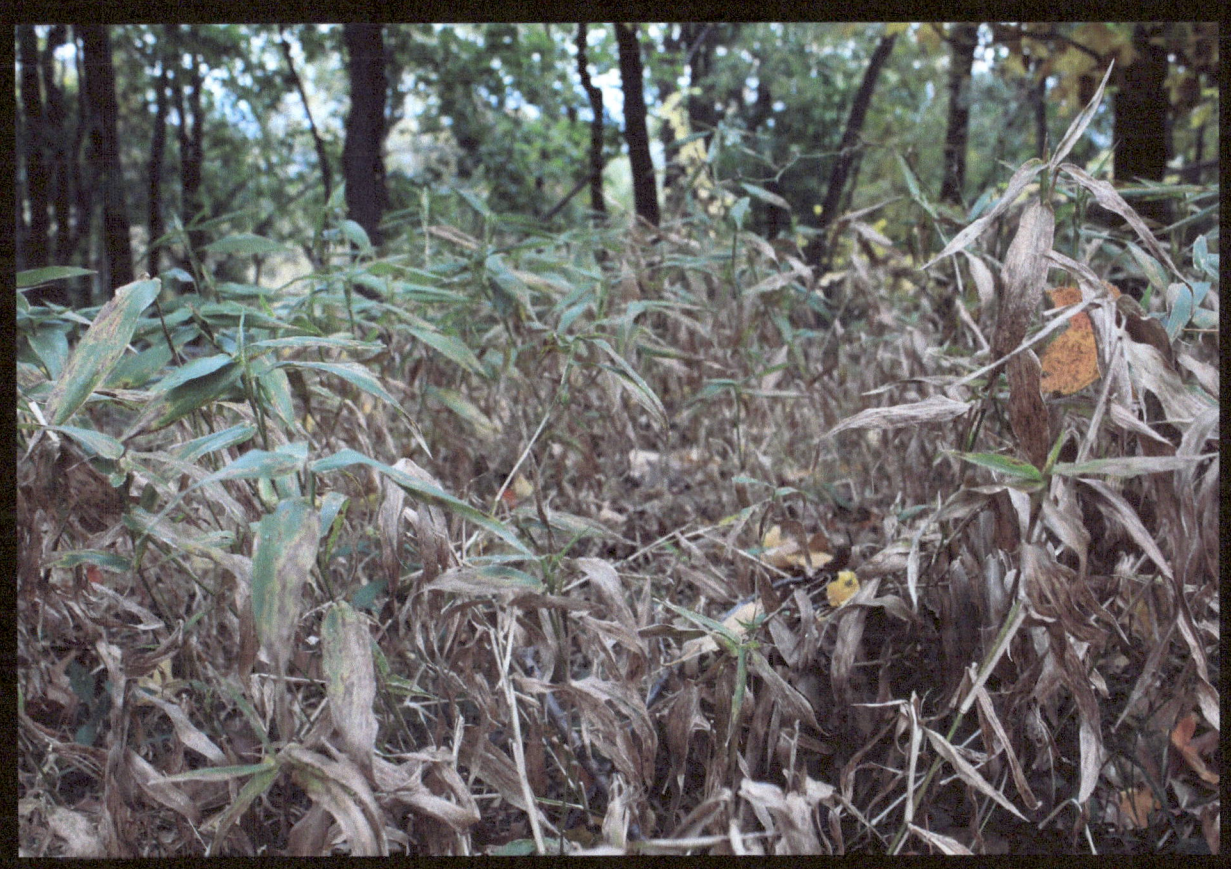

EAGLE ROCK RESERVATION

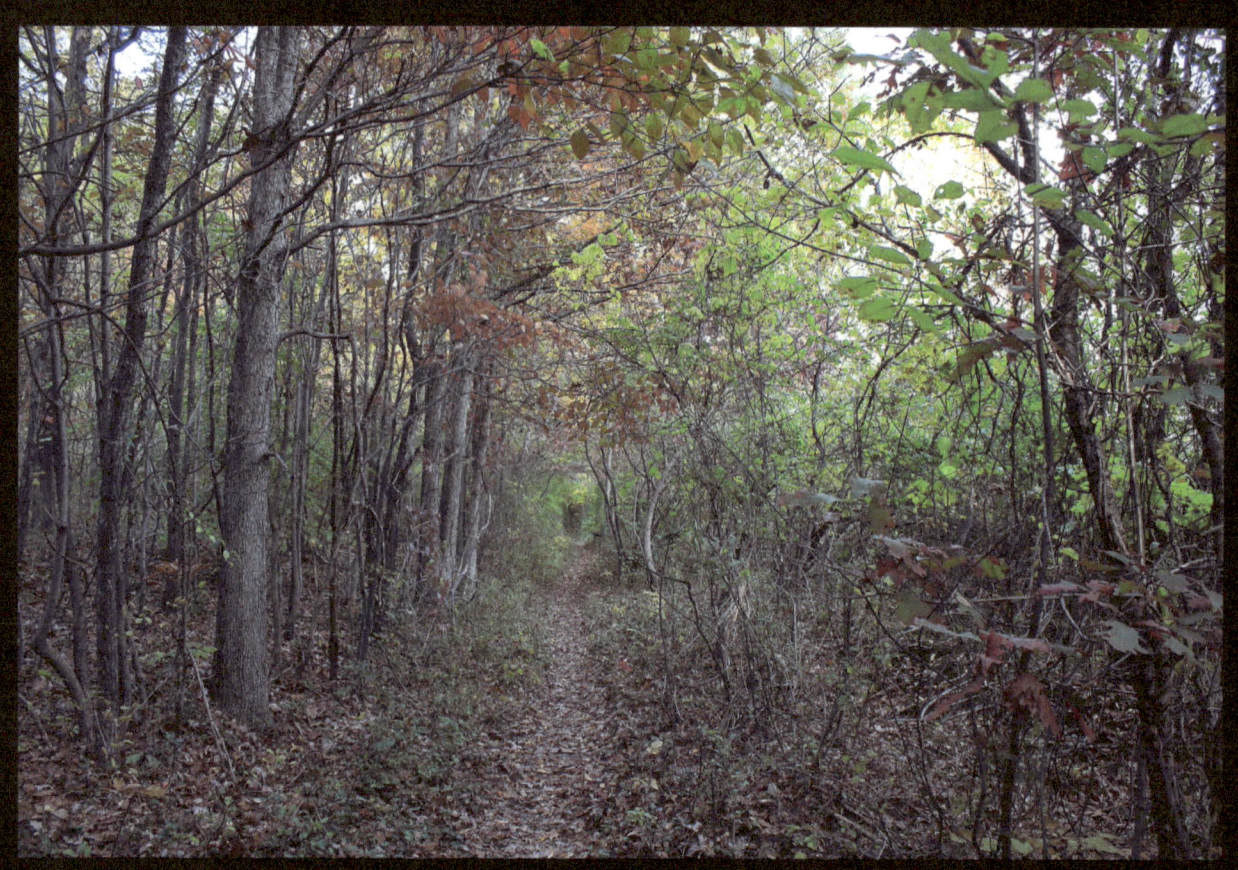

WATCHUNG RESERVATION

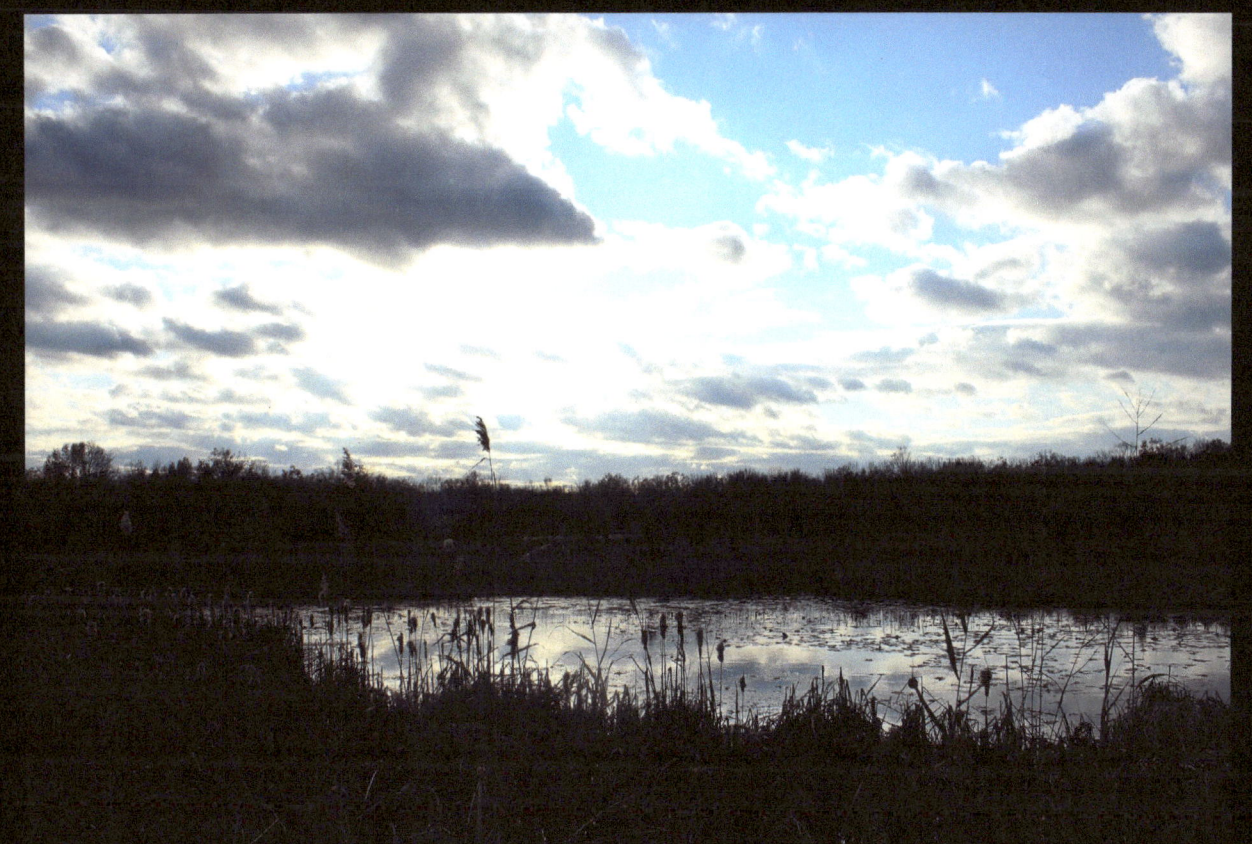

GREAT SWAMP WILDLIFE REFUGE

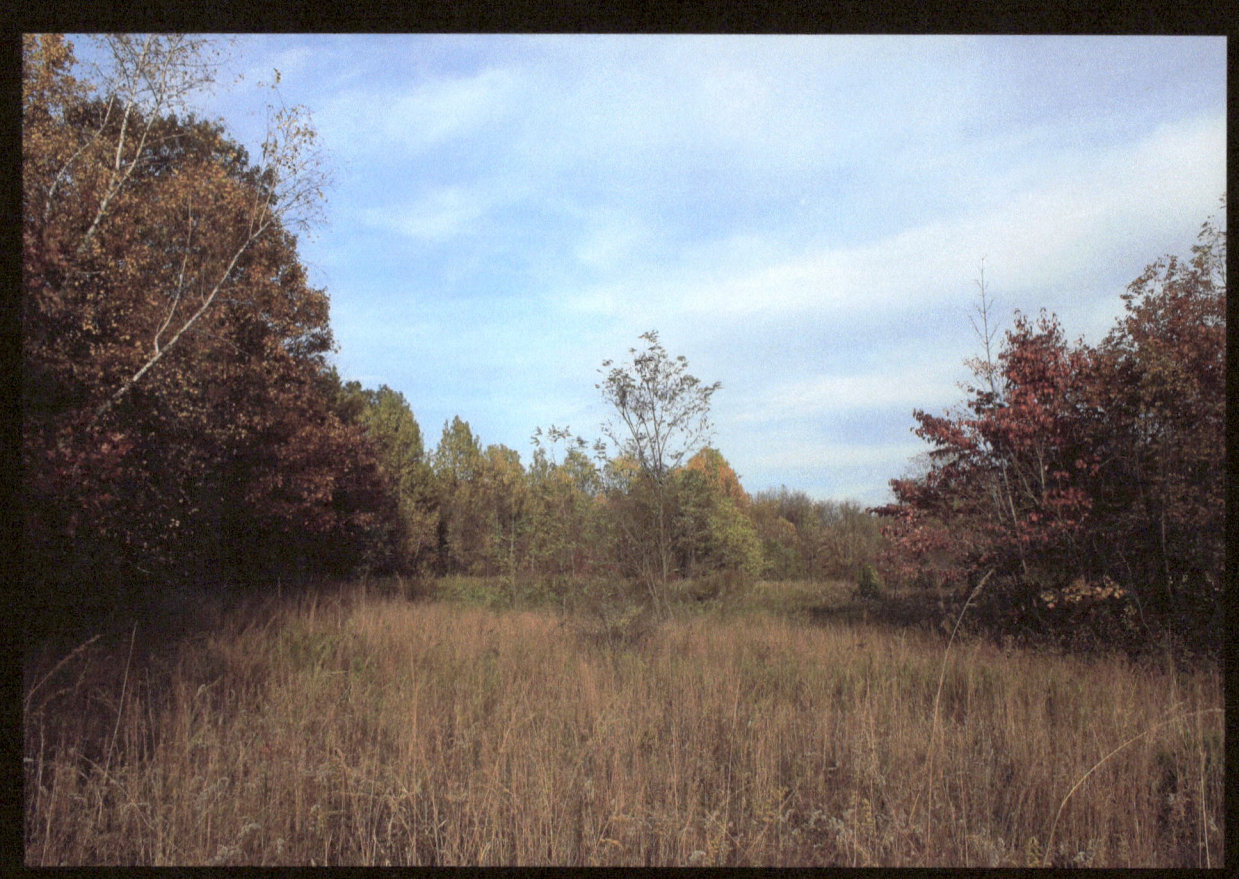

WATCHUNG RESERVATION

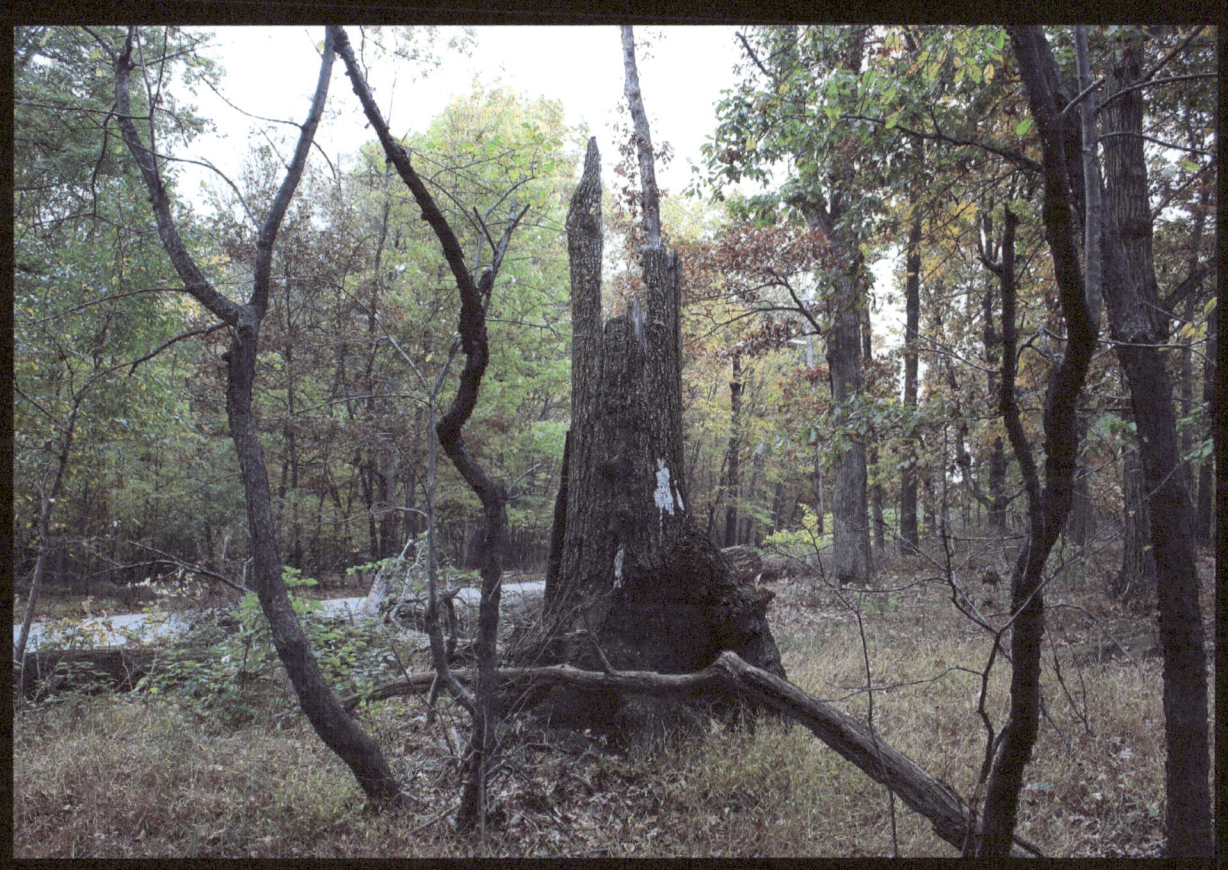

EAGLE ROCK RESERVATION

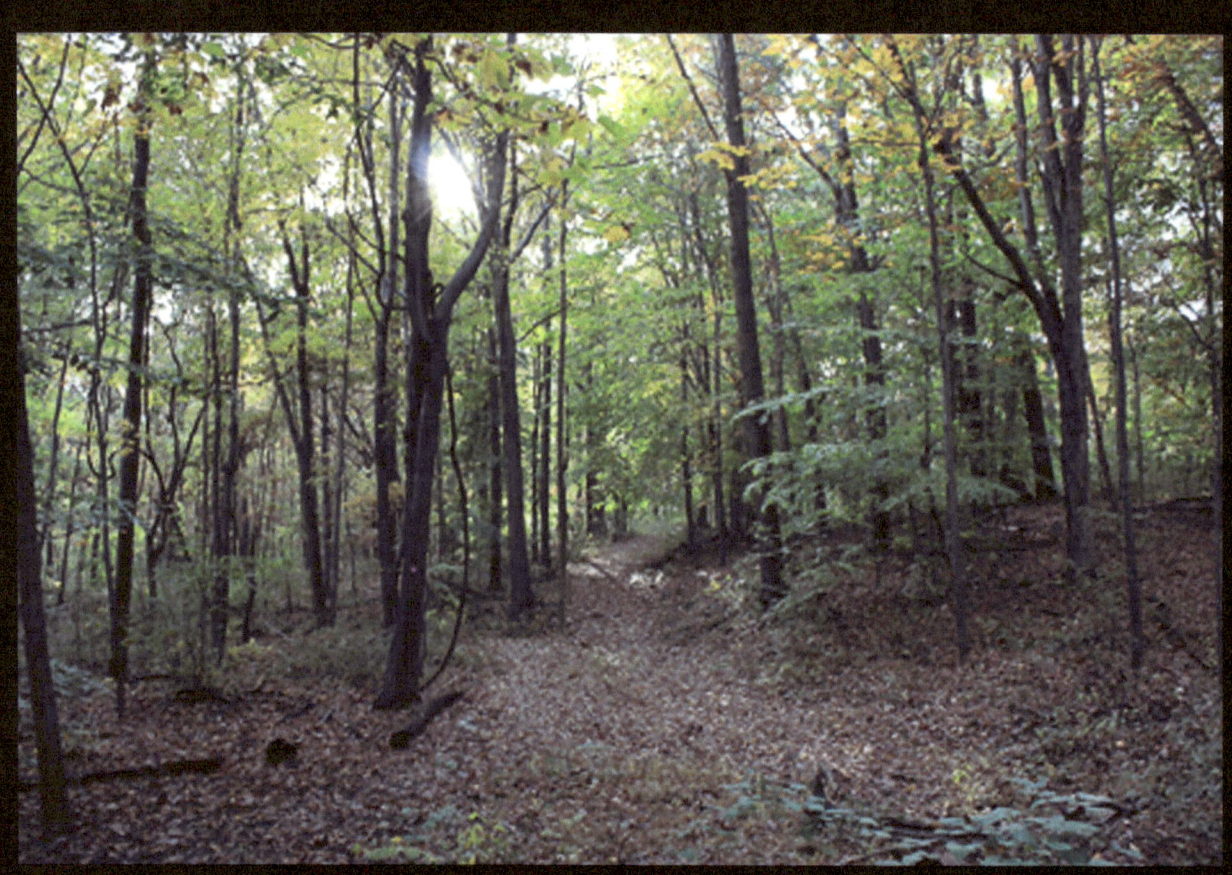

WATCHUNG RESERVATION

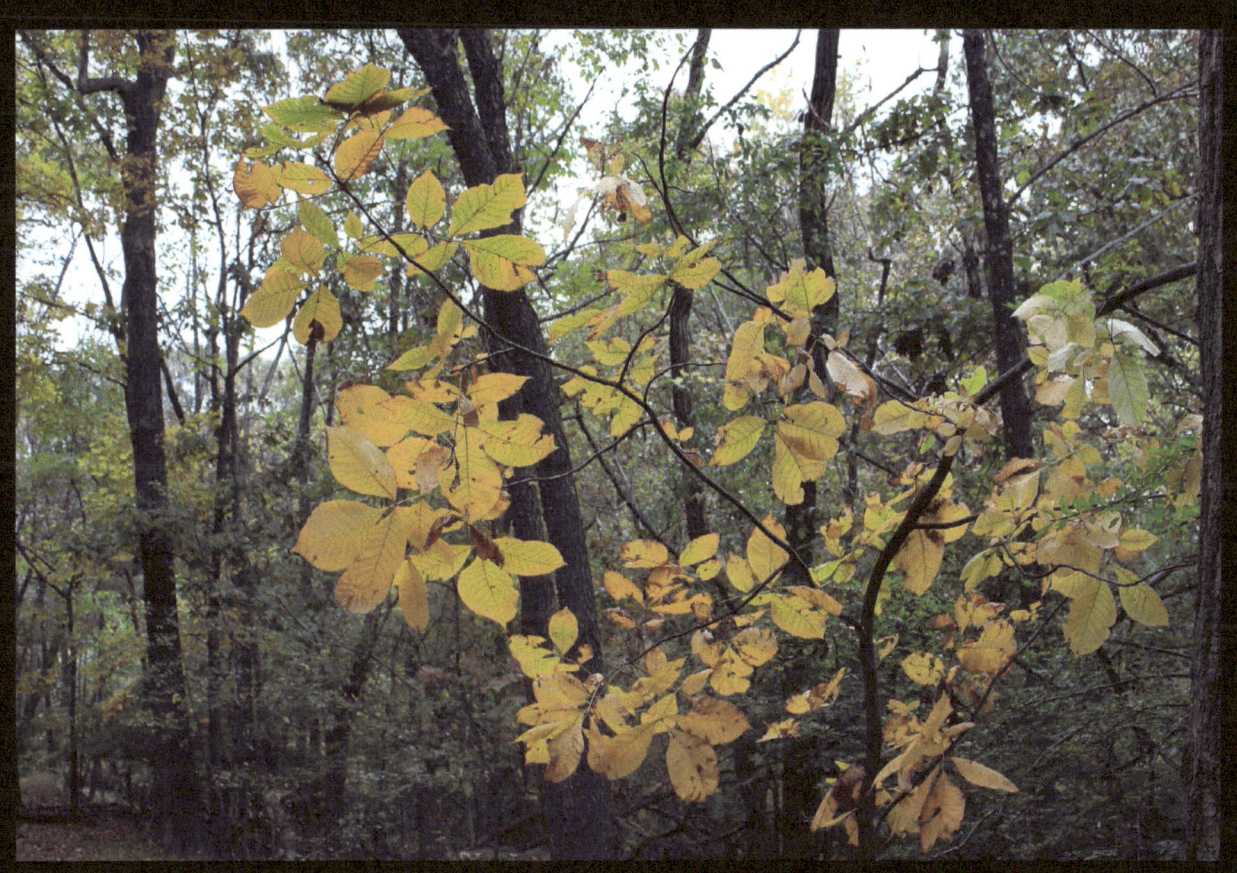

EAGLE ROCK RESERVATION

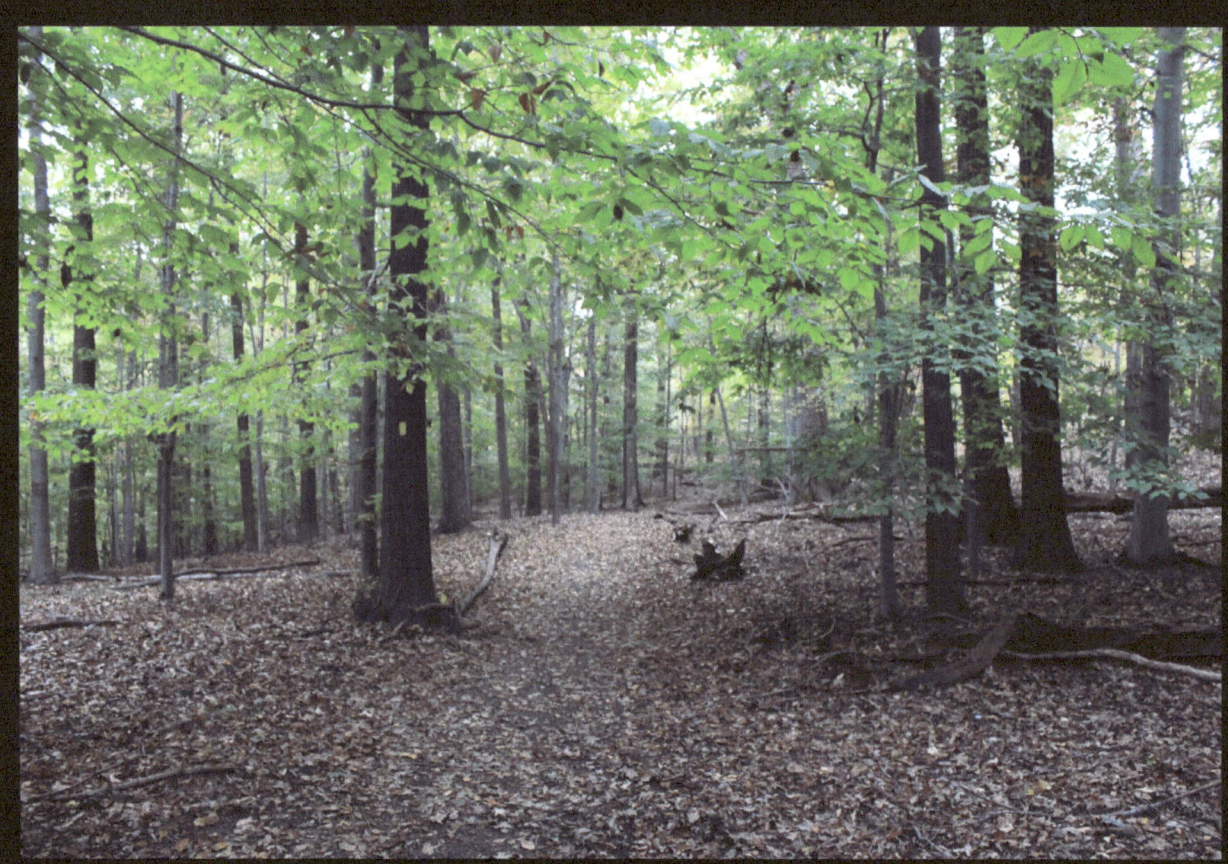

EAGLE ROCK RESERVATION

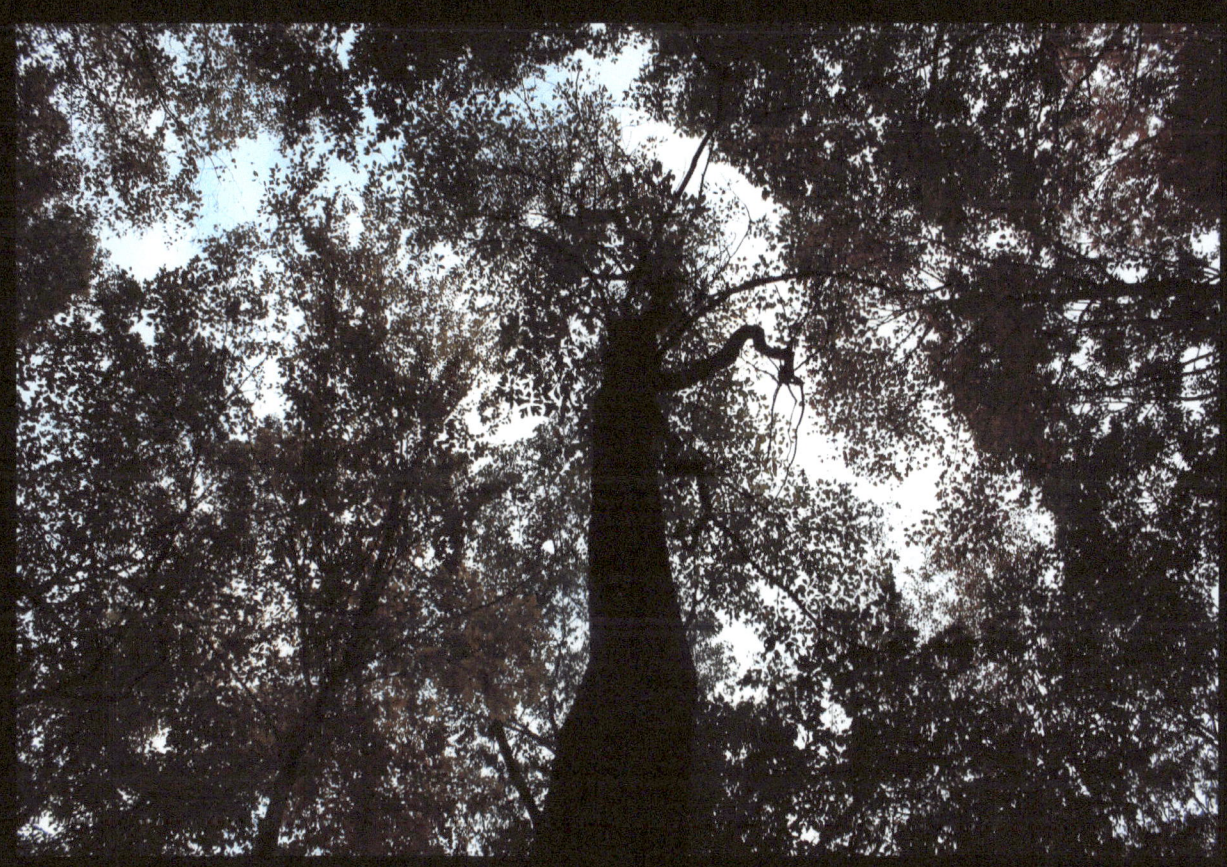

EAGLE ROCK RESERVATION

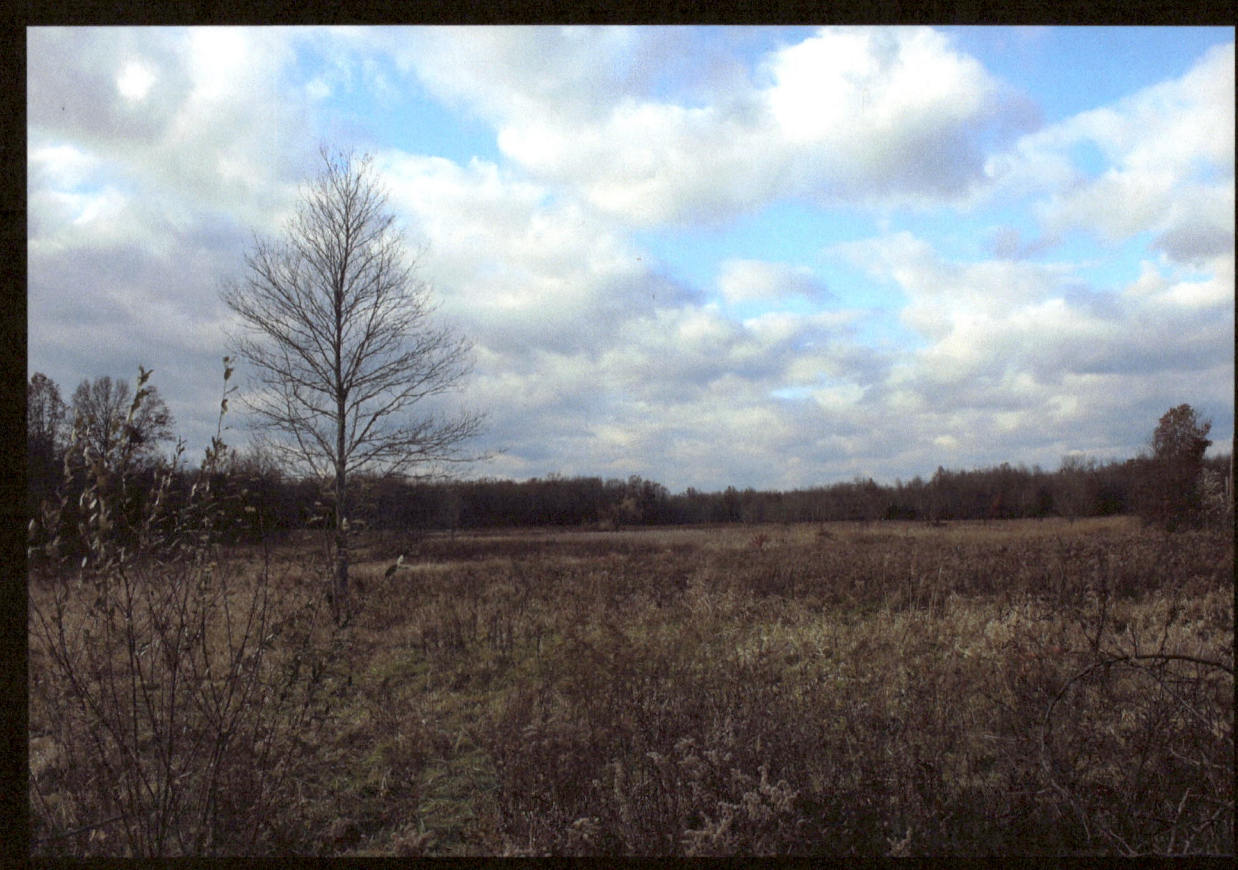

GREAT SWAMP WILDLIFE REFUGE

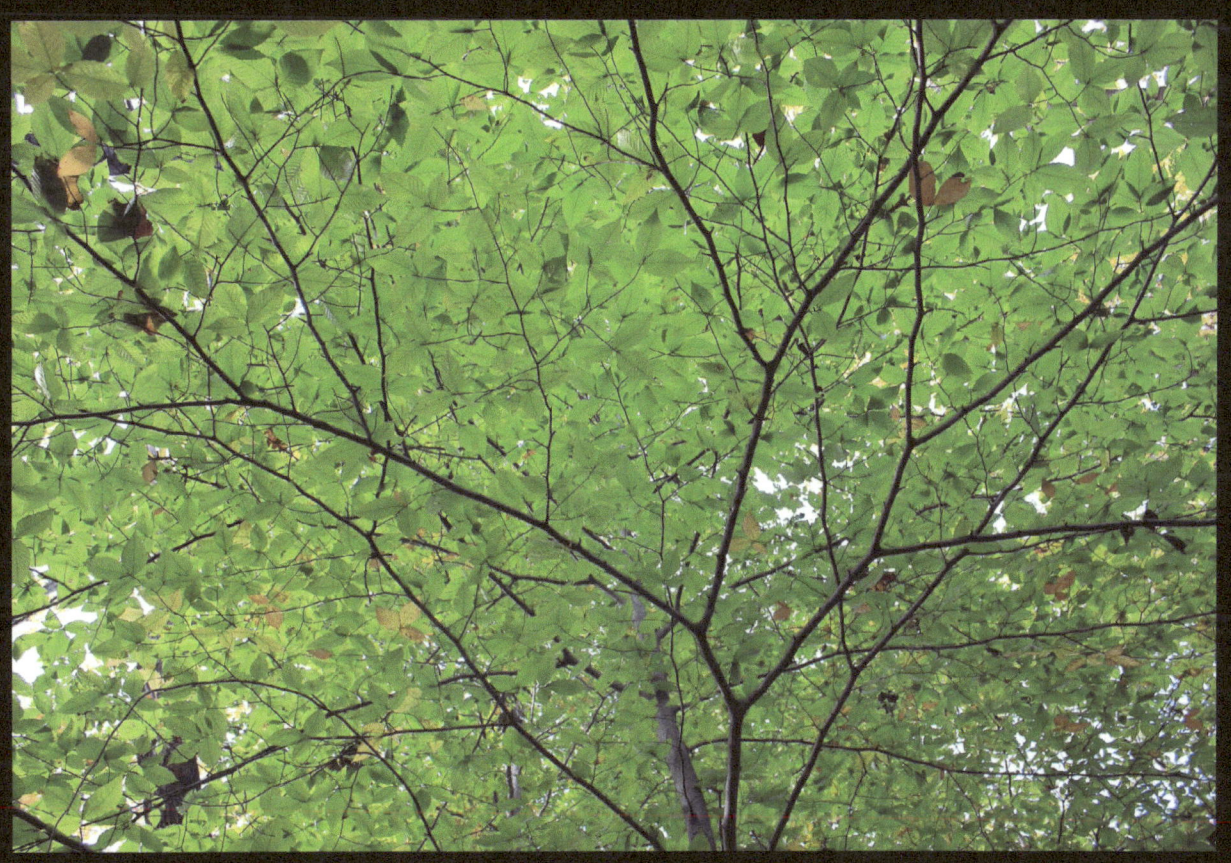

WATCHUNG RESERVATION

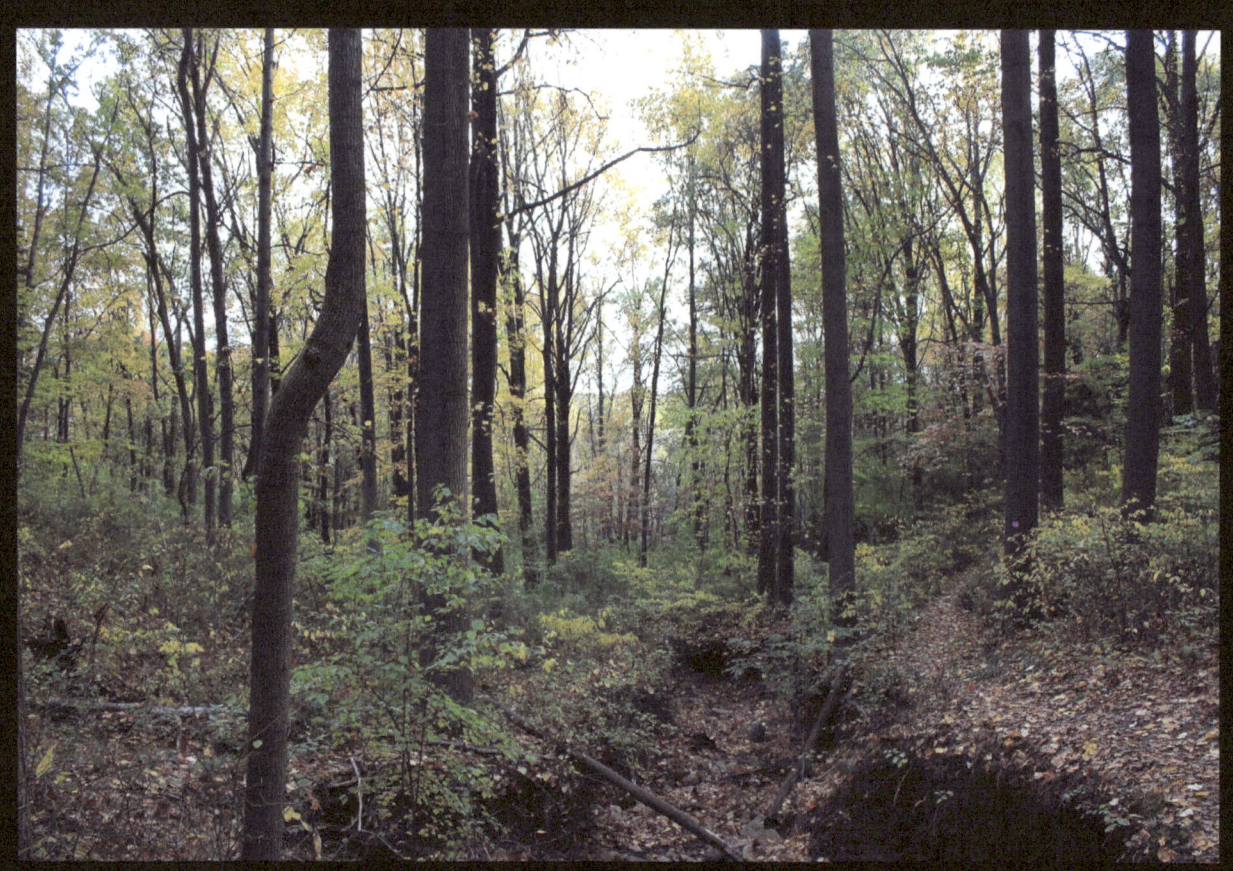

WATCHUNG RESERVATION

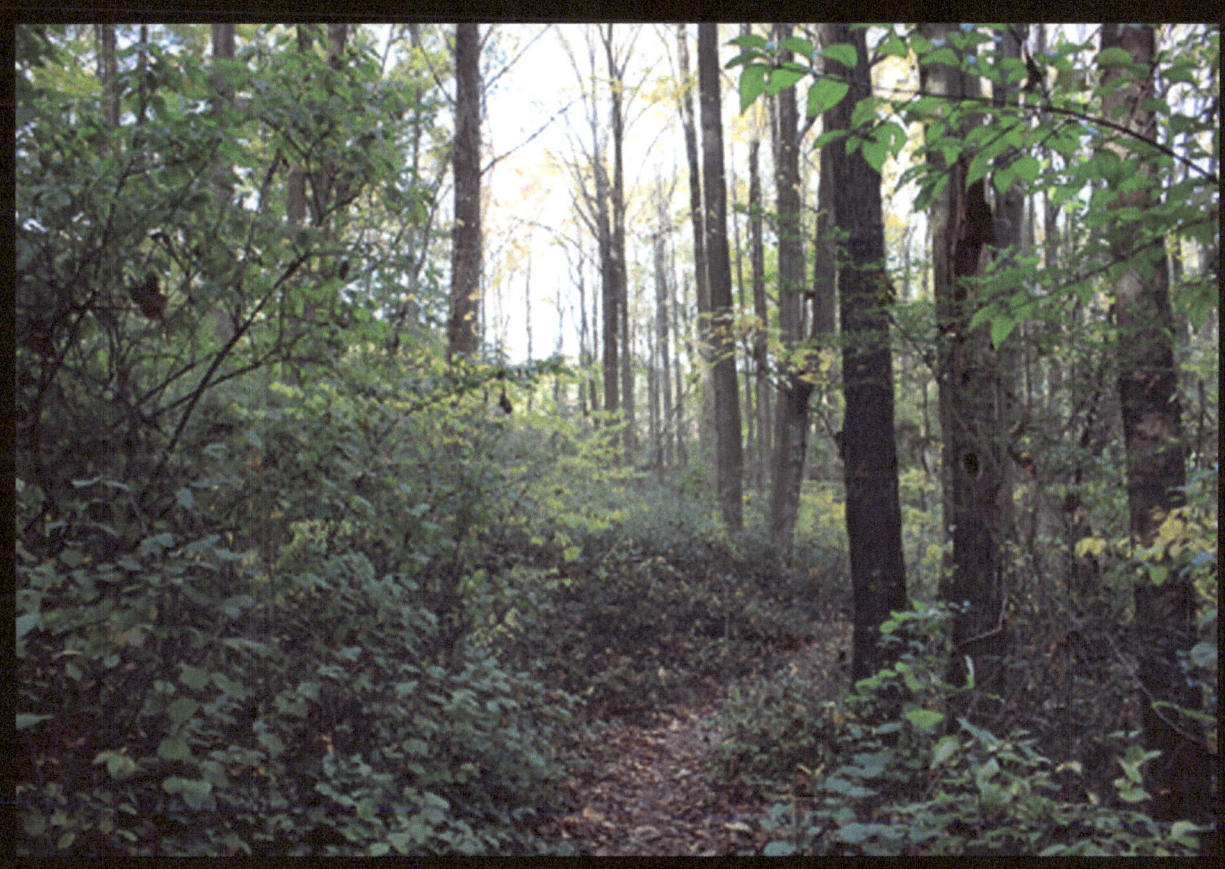

WATCHUNG RESERVATION

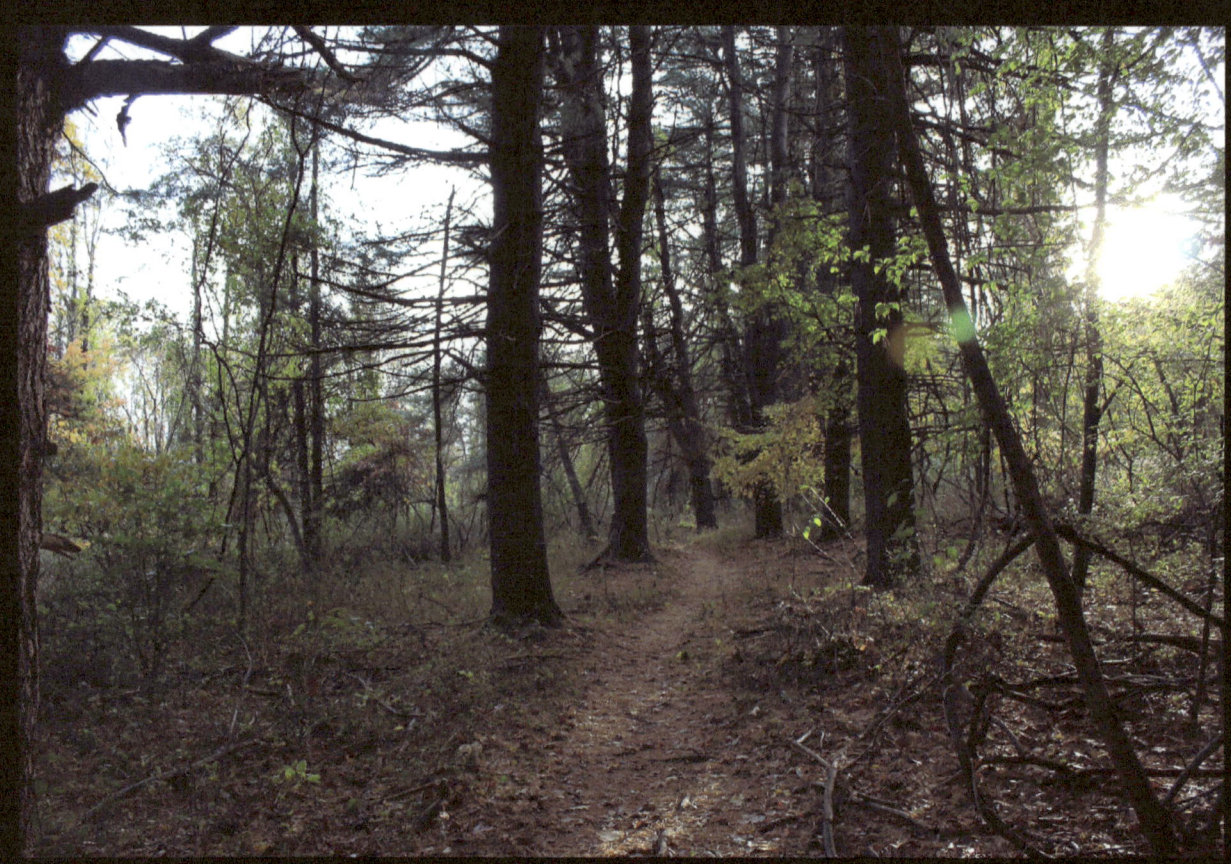

WATCHUNG RESERVATION

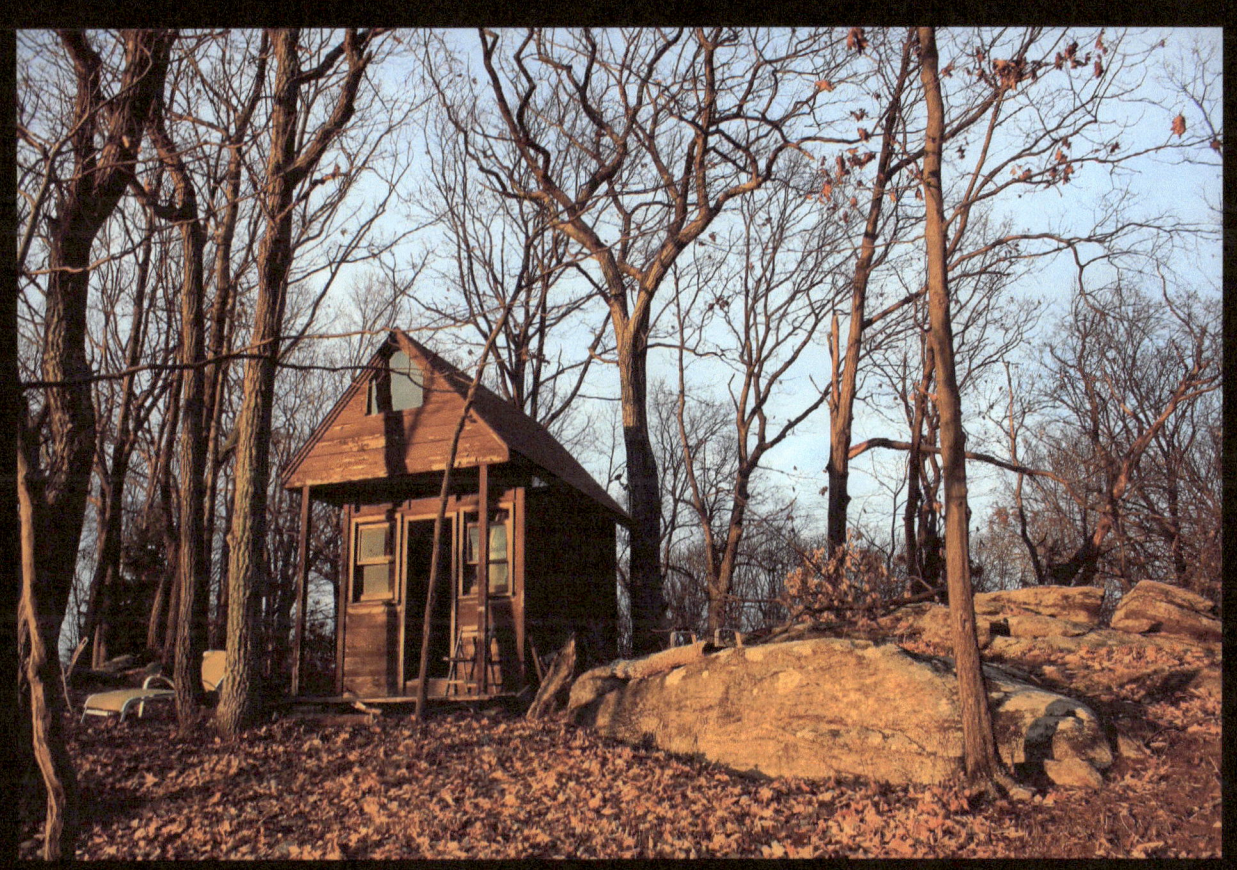

HIGH MOUNTAIN PRESERVE

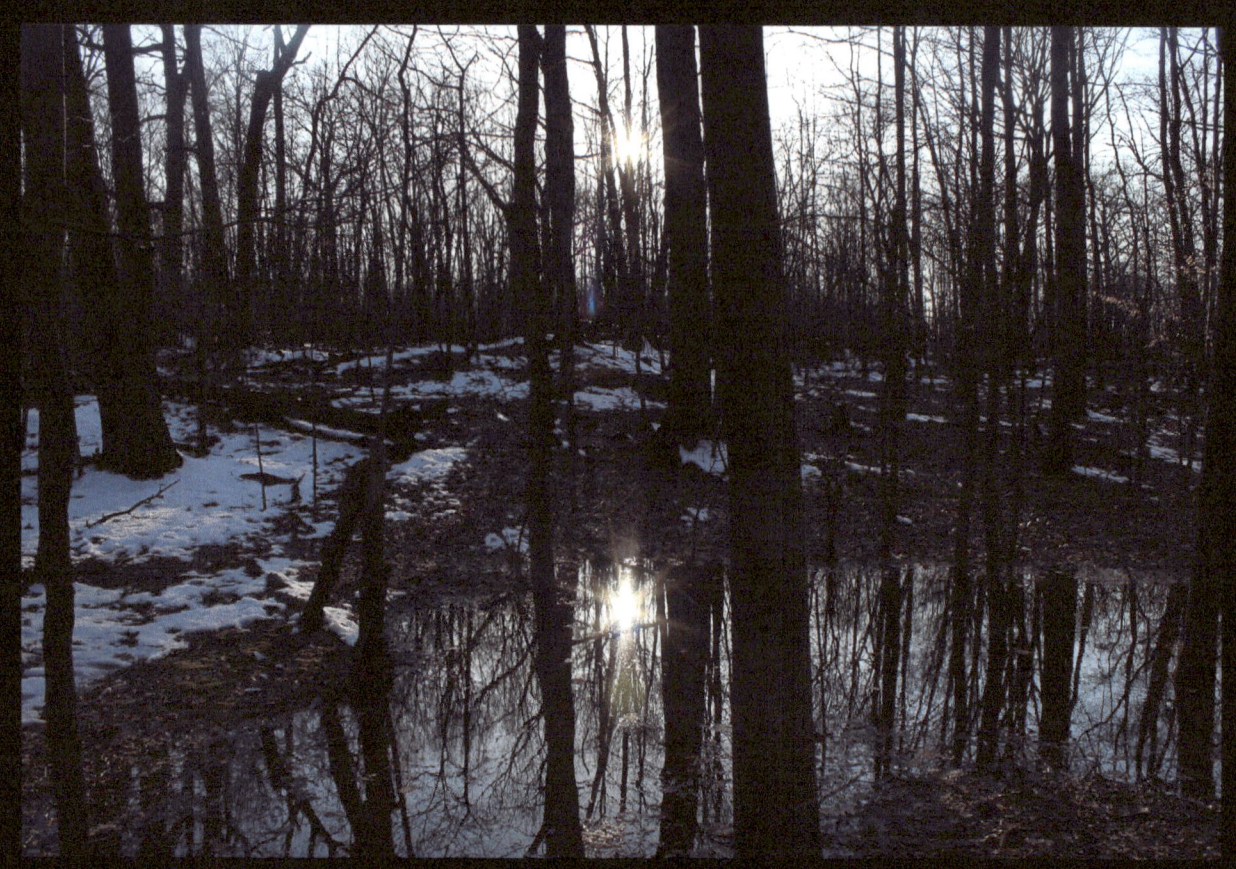

EAGLE ROCK RESERVATION

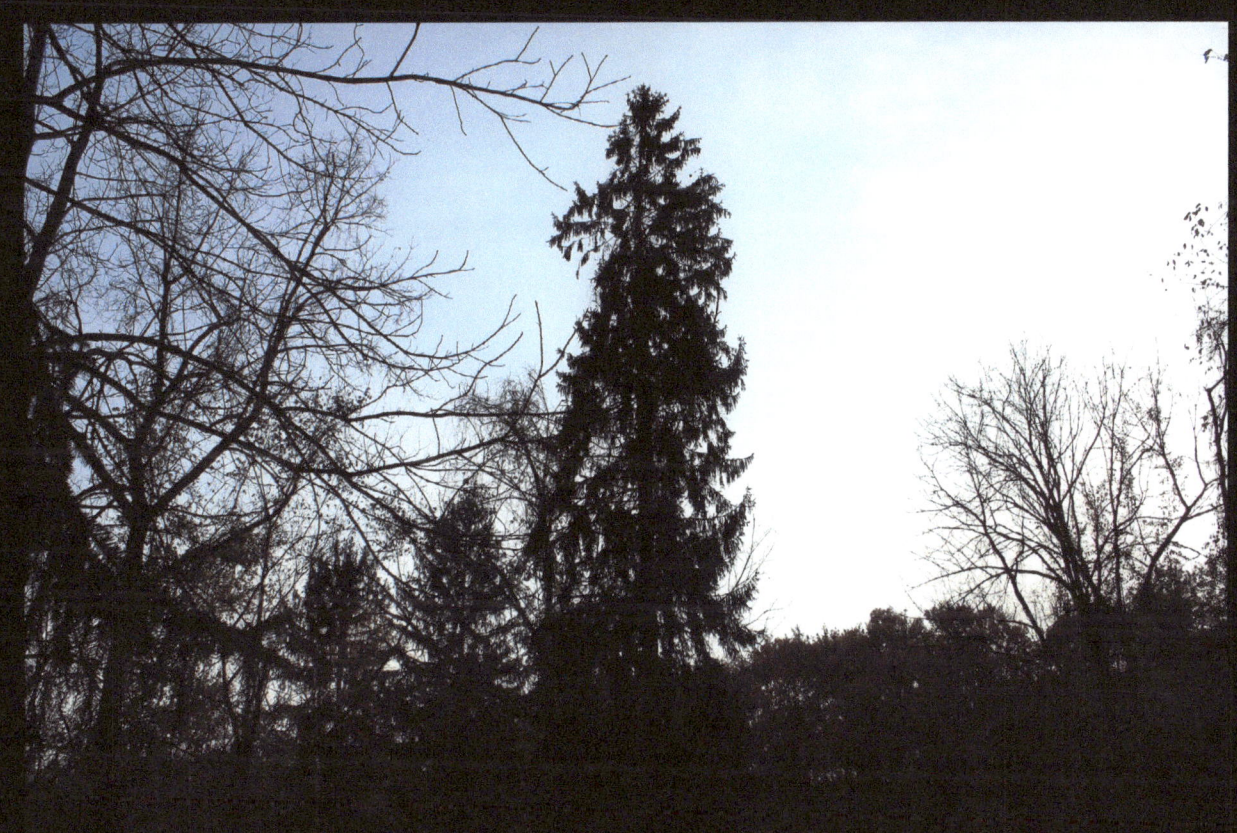

WATCHUNG RESERVATION

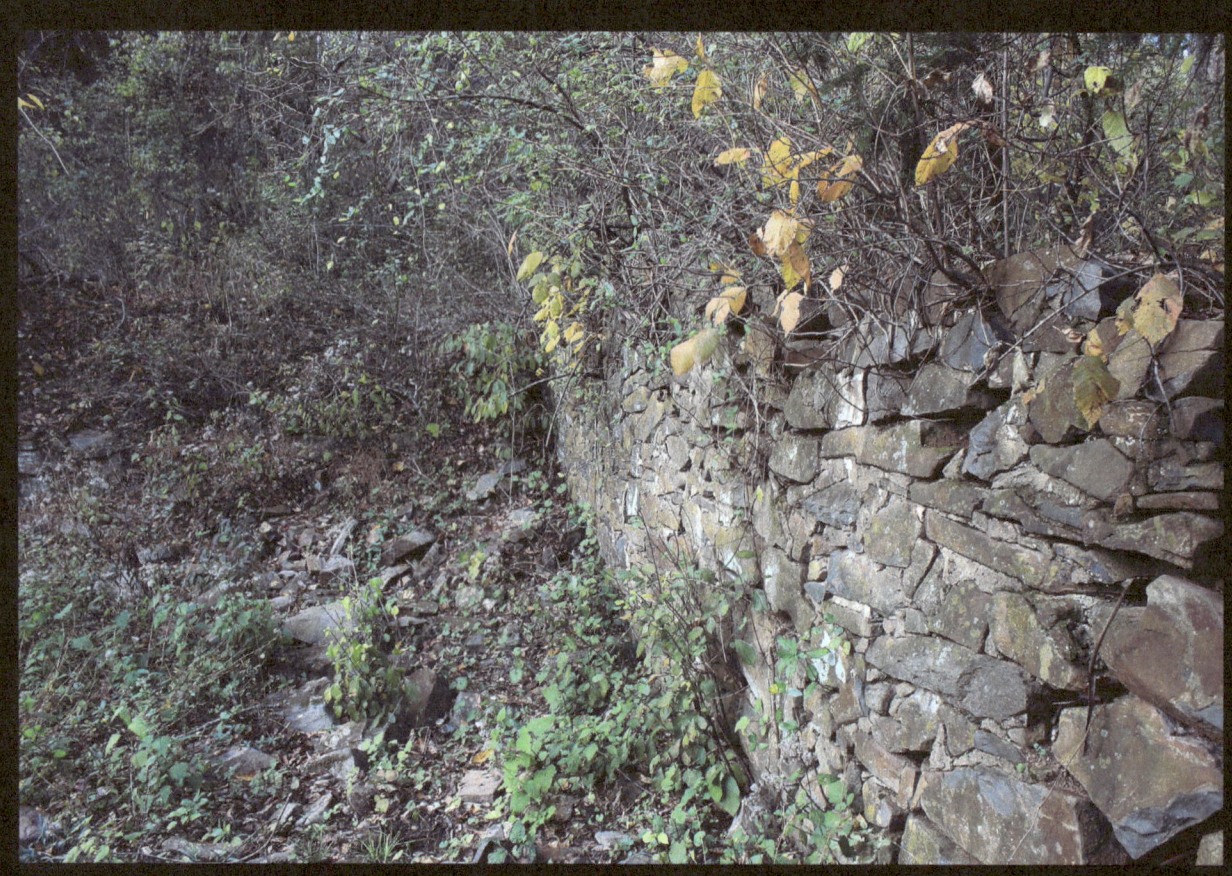

WATCHUNG RESERVATION

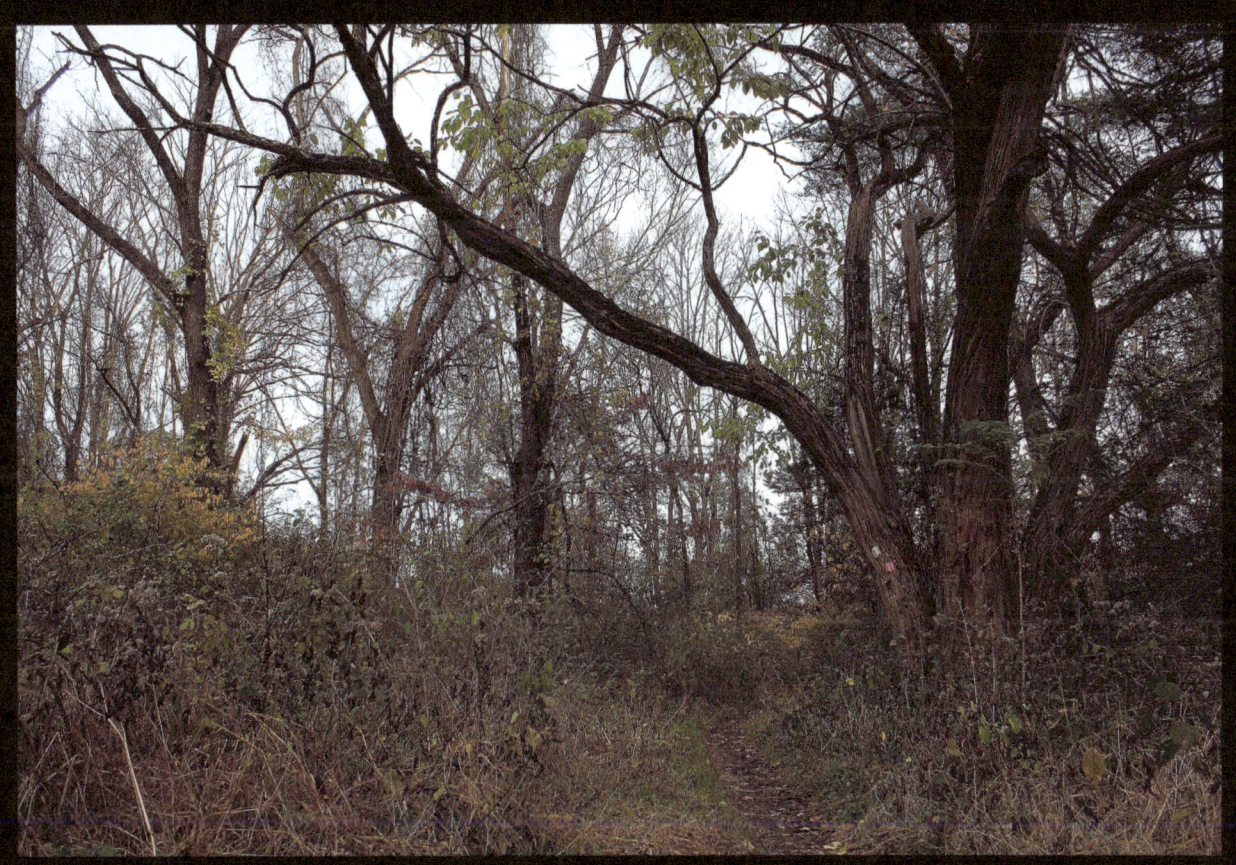

WATCHUNG RESERVATION

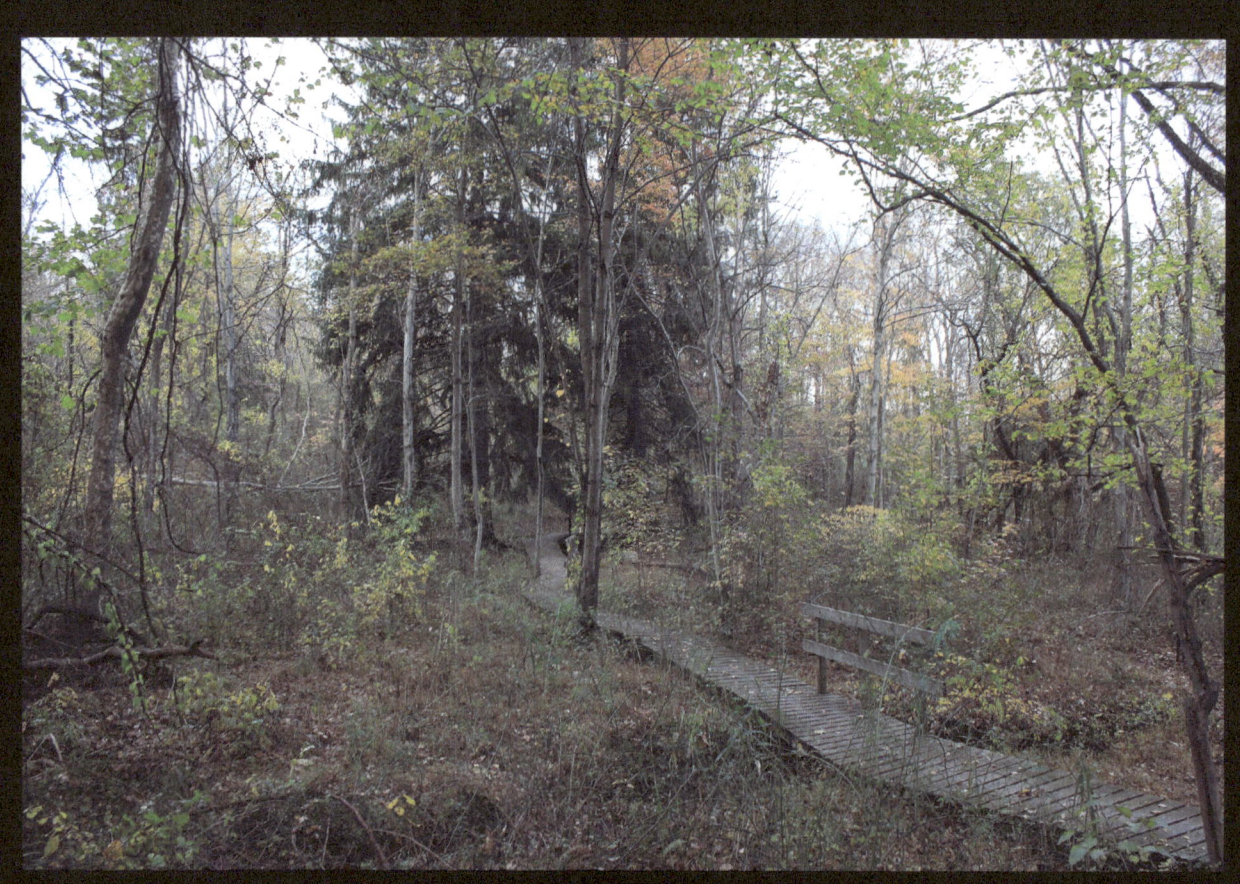

WATCHUNG RESERVATION

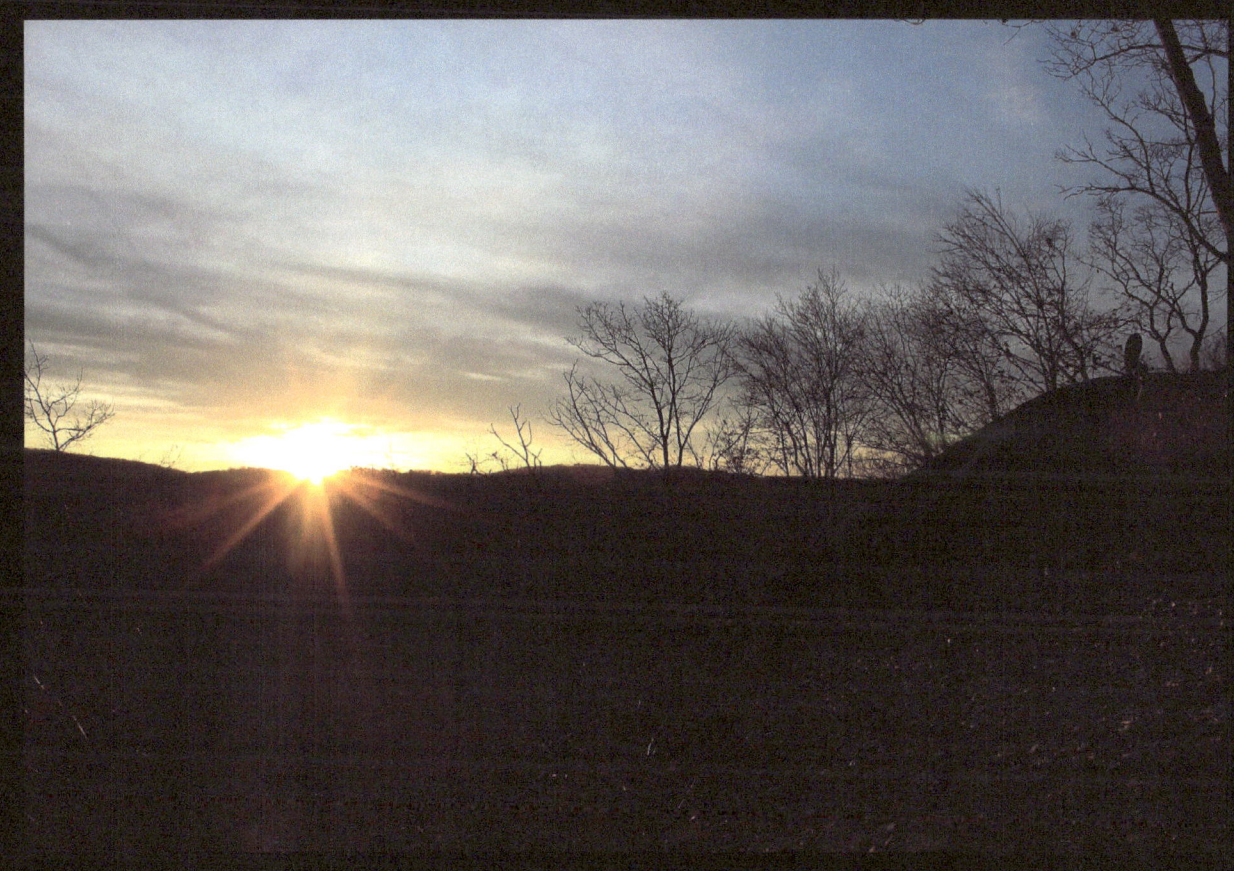

HIGH MOUNTAIN PRESERVE

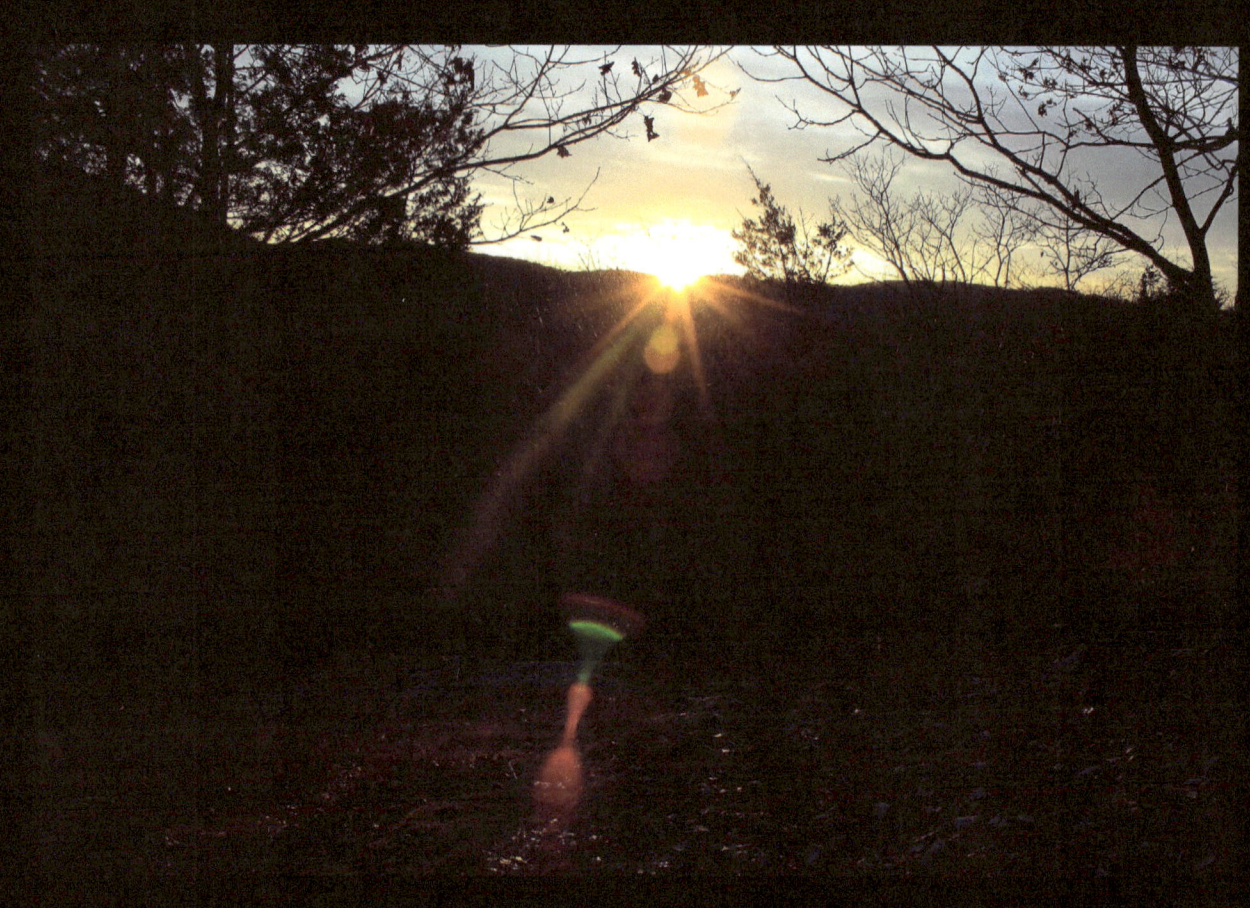

HIGH MOUNTAIN PRESERVE

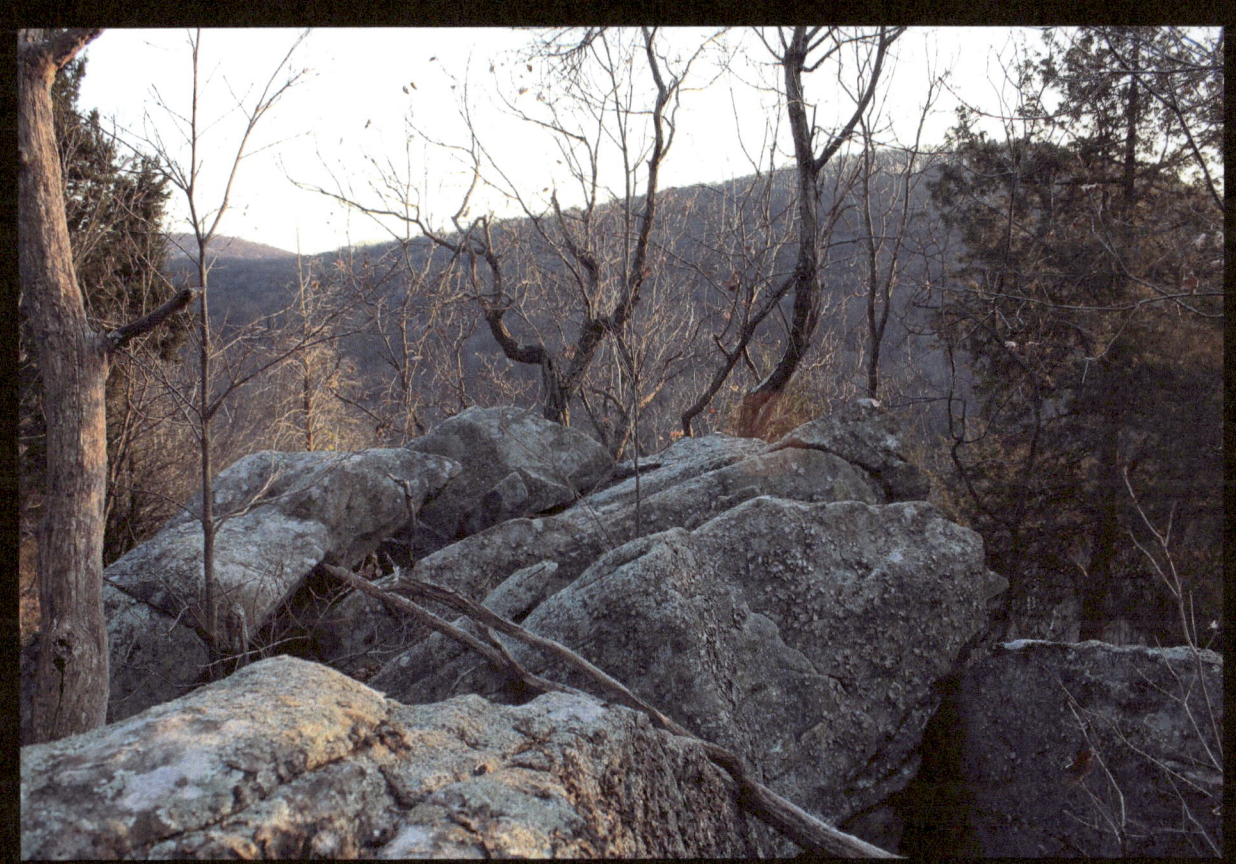

HIGH MOUNTAIN PRESERVE

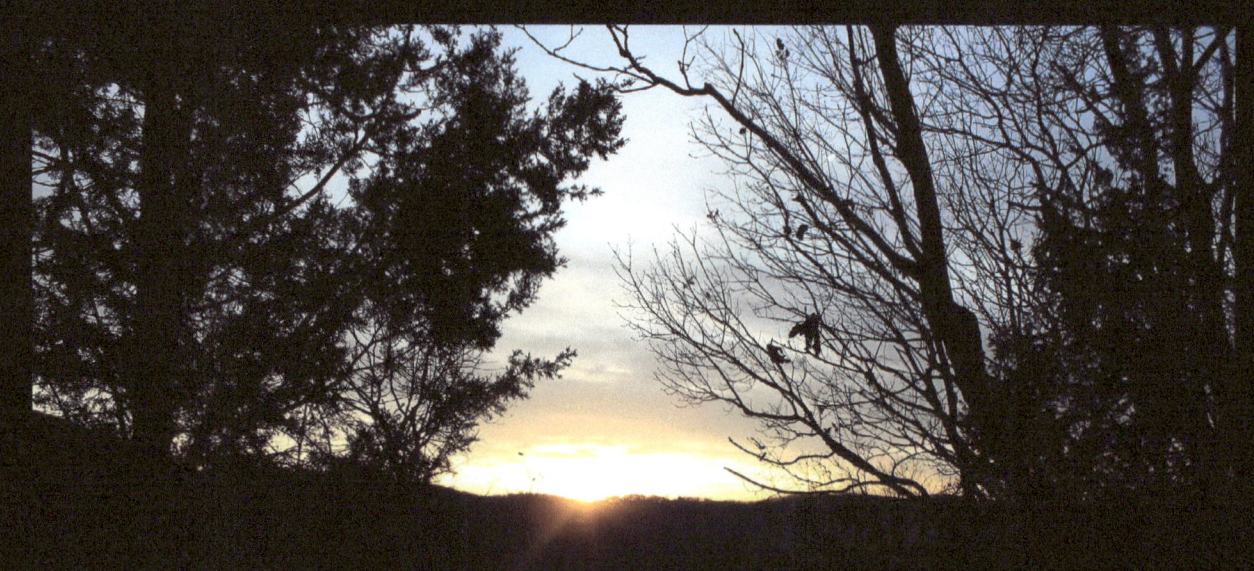

HIGH MOUNTAIN PRESERVE

BLUE HILLS

Dedicated to my grandparents: Frank, Edith, Jim, Diane

During the 17th century, the Quakers bought land across the now Watchung Mountains from the Lenape Tribe in northern New Jersey; they built their houses by hand in the tree tops of the mountains. The high points of elevation within the Watchung Mountains provide people with amazing views of New York City/Hudson River Area. The greatest pleasure that the Quakers shared together was during the mornings; the families would wake up to see a bright blue haze glowing over the tree line in the horizon. From this beautiful blue haze light, the Quakers named the area the "Blue Hills." This project explores the interior and exterior views of the Blue Hills across various parks and national wildlife refuges scattered across the northern area of New Jersey.

www.ingramcontent.com/pod-product-compliance
Lightning Source LLC
Chambersburg PA
CBHW041258180526
45172CB00003B/889